THE POEM OF THE CID

THE POEM OF
THE CID

TRANSLATED BY LESLEY BYRD SIMPSON

UNIVERSITY OF CALIFORNIA PRESS

BERKELEY, LOS ANGELES, AND LONDON

University of California Press
Berkeley and Los Angeles, California

University of California Press, Ltd.
London, England

© 1957, 2006 by
The Regents of the University of California
© renewed 1985 Lesley Byrd Simpson
ISBN 978-0-520-25010-9
Library of Congress Catalog Card Number: 57-10503

Designed by Adrian Wilson

Printed in the United States of America

12   11   10   09   08   07   06

8   7   6   5   4   3   2   1

The paper used in this publication meets the minimum
requirements of ANSI/NISO Z39.48-1992 (R 1997)
(*Permanence of Paper*). ∞

PREFACE

Unique among the heroic poems of the Middle Ages, *The Poem of the Cid*, the national epic of Spain, is remarkable for its vigorous realism and a refreshing absence of that childlike abuse of the marvelous which strains one's credulity to the breaking point in the contemporaneous *Chanson de Roland* and the *Nibelungenlied*. It is, indeed, the earliest extant manifestation of the Spanish genius for realism and robust humor which reached its flower in *Don Quixote de la Mancha*—a "grown-up" outlook on life, as Gerald Brenan calls it, a willingness to face life on its own terms, a lack of cant, an acceptance of unglossed humanity, with its greatness and meanness fairly apportioned.

The hero of the Poem illustrates this very Spanish trait. The Cid lies and cheats, when the occasion demands, in a way which would shock our national myth makers. Where else would a poet dare start his hero off by having him swindle the two Jews, Raquel and Vidas, as the Cid and Martín Antolínez do in the first episode of the Poem? And then have the Cid coolly excuse his felony on the ground that he needed the money!

The Cid is portrayed in all his human aspects. He is, first and always, the ideal Castilian warrior, proud, jealous of his honor, brave and ruthless, delighting in action, vain of his strength and skill, given to innocent boasting ("I am Ruy Díaz, the Cid, he of Bivar!"), reveling in bloodshed; but he is shrewd and generous, a born leader of men and a cunning tactician, scornful of weakness and poltroonery, magnanimous in victory, and, with it all, pious, sentimental about his family, loyal to his companions and even to his King (although one may suspect that the Cid's loyalty to Alfonso, too frequently expressed, like that of Hernán Cortés to the Emperor Charles V in a similar situation, is not unmixed with prudence), and, finally, he is endowed with a saving peasant humor. The poet, naturally, makes the most of his hero's virtues. To him Ruy Díaz is almost always "My" Cid. His admiration bursts forth in frequent epithet: "The loyal Campeador," "he of the noble beard," "he who won Valencia," and, every few lines, the persuasive and hypnotic chant, "he who in a happy hour was born." So intimately does the poet identify himself with his subject that he assumes the part of a participant in the events he describes, or that of the reader in a puppet show (like Master Peter's boy in *Don Quixote*) and urges us to share his excitement in the stirring recital.

He treats the Cid's lieutenants with the same delighted enthusiasm and never wearies of calling their glorious roll. "Ah, how well does My Cid Ruy Díaz the good fighter do battle from his gilded saddle! And Minaya Alvar Fáñez, who commanded at Zorita! And Martín Antolínez, that noble son of Burgos! And Muño Gustioz, that servant of the Cid! And Martín Muñoz, who commanded at Monte Mayor! And Alvar Alvarez! And Alvar Salvadórez! And Galindo García, the good Aragonese! And Félix Muñoz, that nephew of the Campeador!"

The poet is equally charmed by the sonorous place names of Spain: San Esteban "that good city," Alcubilla, Quinea, Navapalos, Figueruela, Sierra de Miedes, Atienza "held by the Moors," Alcalá, Castejón, Guadalajara, Alhama, La Hoz, Briviesca, Ateca, Alcocer, Calatayud, Huesa, Montalbán. . . . No matter who is traveling— and the Poem is a constant movement—the places along the way are recited in a lingering litany. The poet loved his country and loved the *sound* of his country.

The Poem of the Cid, according to its great editor and historian, Ramón Menéndez Pidal, was composed about 1140, that is, less than half a century after the Cid's death in 1099. The only copy of it that has survived has 3,730 verses. It was made in 1307 by a certain Pedro Abbat and by some miracle was preserved in the local archives of Bivar, near Burgos, where it lay forgotten for almost five centuries, until it was published in 1779 by Tomás Antonio Sánchez. The Abbat MS lacks three folios: the first, and two in the third canto. Menéndez Pidal has supplied these gaps by drawing upon the thirteenth century *Crónica de los veynte reyes de Castilla,* which is almost certainly a prose rendition of the Poem. I have adopted his interpolations in the third canto, setting them off in square brackets, but have reduced the first to a paragraph in my Argument of the Poem, because its wordiness seems to me at odds with the economy characteristic of the poet. The loss of the first folio may, indeed, be a happy accident, for a more effective beginning than the first line of the Abbat MS can hardly be imagined:

De los sos ojos tan fuertemientre llorando,

which plunges us at once into the most intimate mood of the Poem.

ARGUMENT OF THE POEM

According to the *Crónica de los veynte reyes,* just mentioned, Ruy Díaz de Bivar, called the Cid Campeador, has been sent by King Alfonso of León and Castile to collect the annual tribute owed him by the Moorish King of Seville. In Seville the Cid learns that the King of Granada, aided by a group of Leonese nobles commanded by Count García Ordóñez, is making war upon the King of Seville. Now, since the King of Seville is a tributary of King Alfonso, the Cid Campeador takes it upon himself to lead a punitive expedition against the King of Granada and his allies. He meets them at the castle of Cabra and administers a resounding defeat, taking Count García Ordóñez prisoner and plucking his beard for good measure, the unforgivable insult.

Not unexpectedly, therefore, the count becomes the Cid's "wicked enemy" and misses no opportunity to embroil him with King Alfonso. He easily persuades the King that the Cid is becoming dangerously powerful and even plans to kill him, so the King summarily banishes the Cid from his kingdom. Here begins the Poem proper of the Abbat MS, with the departure of the Cid from Bivar accompanied by the sixty knights of his household.

Canto One, "The Exile," relates the Cid's forays into Moorish territory in quest of booty with which to attract more men to his standard and to begin his long task of winning back the King's favor by showering him with gifts, while Count García does his utmost to keep the King's wrath stirred up against his great vassal. The Cid fights his way clear to the eastern side of the peninsula, where he runs foul of Ramón Berenguer, Count of Barcelona. The canto ends with the count's defeat and the comical episode of his hunger strike.

In Canto Two, "The Wedding," the Cid continues his spectacular career of conquest, even taking the city of Valencia. He makes himself "king" of the city and exercises his new authority by appointing Jerome, "that good Christian," Bishop of Valencia, who divides his time nicely between saying Mass and slaying Moors, "for the honor of his order." The Cid, now immensely rich, with a private army of 3,600, again sends his "right arm," Alvar Fáñez, to King Alfonso with such a huge gift that the King visibly softens and grants him permission to bring his wife and daughters to Valencia. Impressed with the Cid's growing power and wealth, the young Princes (*Infantes*) of Carrión conceive the unlucky notion of marrying the Cid's daughters, "for their profit." A third thumping gift induces the King to pardon the Cid, and as a further honor and proof of his affection he undertakes to arrange the marriage of the Cid's daughters to the Princes of Carrión. The reconciliation between the King and the Cid is celebrated with great pomp and rejoicing on the banks of the Tagus, and is sealed by the formal betrothal of the Cid's daughters. The Cid brings the Princes of Carrión to his kingdom of Valencia and there, in a gay festival that lasts a fortnight, the Cid's daughters are married. The Cid rejoices to see his honor increased by this union with the noble family of the Beni-Gómez.

Canto Three, "The Outrage at Corpes," begins with the absurd episode of the escape of the Cid's pet lion, in which the Cid's new sons-in-law show themselves to be arrant cowards, one of them hiding in terror beneath the bench upon which the Cid is sleeping, the other taking refuge behind the wine press in very harrowing circumstances. Fernando González, one of the princes, further disgraces himself by turning tail in battle, although he is shielded from exposure at the time by the good-natured Pedro Bermúdez, the Cid's standard-bearer. Smarting from the ridicule of which they are now the butt, the Princes of Carrión plot a disgusting revenge.

They obtain the Cid's permission to bring their wives to Carrión and, upon the way, in the "oaken woods of Corpes," they strip them and whip them and leave them for dead.

Luckily, the Cid, belatedly uneasy about his daughters' marriage, has sent his nephew, Félix Muñoz, along with his daughters. The faithful Félix, who shares his lord's uneasiness, slips away from the princes' company, follows their track to the woods of Corpes, and there discovers his cousins' apparently lifeless bodies bathed in blood. He rescues them, and soon the whole country knows of the foul deed. The Cid demands that the King bring the Princes of Carrión to trial, and the King, now wholly won over to the Cid's camp, does so. The princes receive the full measure of justice, including a ridiculously unequal combat with two of the Cid's most redoubtable warriors, Pedro Bermúdez and Martín Antolínez. Poetic justice is further served when the rulers of Navarre and Aragón send their ambassadors to the court, begging the hands of the Cid's daughters in marriage. Thus the Cid's tarnished honor is restored and his enemies are put to shame. As the delighted poet exclaims, at the end of the Poem: "See how his honor increases, he who in a happy hour was born, for the Kings of Spain are now among his kinsmen!"

Such is the simple frame upon which the poet hangs his tapestry. But what a tapestry! At his magic touch, the people, the landscape, the pageantry, the vivid colors, the movement of the Poem, come to life, and all this in a vocabulary of 1,200 words!

The poet tells his story in irregular alexan-
drines, broken into well-marked distichs, each
with a single strong stress. His rhyme scheme is
assonance, the classical assonance of Spanish bal-
ladry, that is, an agreement of the final two
vowels, or, when the verses end in a stressed
vowel, the final vowels alone. The Poem is di-
vided into 152 stanzas, or rather, changes of as-
sonance, having nothing to do with topics, being
merely a device to avoid monotony. The cantos,
on the other hand, represent the three major
episodes in the Cid's long climb back into royal
favor, and reach their climax with his final tri-
umph. The Poem is a fine piece of architecture.

The poet relies for musical effect upon his
long cadences and thus gains freedom from the
asphyxiating regularity which quite ruined the
poetry of Spain in the following century. The
vast superiority of his prosody becomes at once
apparent if we compare his verses with those of
his most prolific successor, Gonzalo de Berceo,
who wrote endlessly in his *nueva maestría*, or
new method, a hundred years later. Take the
opening quatrain of the Poem, for example,

De los sos ojos / tan fuertemientre llorando,
tornaba la cabeza / i estabalos catando.
Vio puertas abiertas / e uços sin cañados,
alcandaras vazias / sin pielles e sin mantos . . . ,

and compare it with this doggerel of Berceo's,

Quiero fer una prosa / en roman paladino,
en qual suele el pueblo / fablar a su vezino,

ca non so tan letrado / por fer otro latino.
Bien valdra commo creo / un vaso de bon vino.

There is no English verse form, to my knowledge, which even remotely suggests the rhythm of *The Poem of the Cid*. None of the three translations succeeds in capturing the flavor of the original, for when the free-flowing line of the Poem is forced into a quantitative strait jacket, its beauty is somehow sacrificed. I shall not labor the matter, but, until some great poet hits upon the secret, it occurred to me that a simple prose rendition, sticking pretty close to the narrative, might give the English reader a better notion of what the grand old Poem is like, and this is what I have done.

An immense amount of ink has been spilled by scholars during the past century over the historicity of the Poem, and especially over the character of the Cid himself. Fortunately, it is needless to review the controversy, for the monumental work of Ramón Menéndez Pidal has settled, probably for all time, every point worthy of argument, and the Cid now occupies his rightful niche in the history of Spain as the greatest figure of his age, entirely deserving of the popular adulation which in later centuries built up about his name a fine collection of ballads, few of them, to be sure, based upon fact. The Poem itself is generally much closer to verifiable history. But all that, I submit, is beside the point, which is that the poet was only concerned with the artistic fidelity of his work. He seized upon the age-old feud between the arrogant nobility of León and the upstart Castilian knights who, more often than not, owned nothing but a horse, a lance, and a coat of mail, and made a precarious living as mercenaries in the pay of Moors and Christians indifferently. The poet personified the feud in Count García Ordóñez and the Beni-Gómez clan of Carrión, on the one side, and the Cid and his knights, on the other, set King Alfonso on top of the heap, and worked out his plot with an eye to pleasing his Castilian listeners. He distorts, amplifies, excludes, telescopes, and invents, bringing in identifiable figures, places, and episodes to lend a specious authority to his tale.

The poet is hotly partisan and makes no pretense of giving the enemy a fair break. The invention of the outrage of the Cid's daughters is a thoroughly nasty piece of hatefulness, and incredible besides. Evidently meant as an antithesis for the Cid's nobility, it is no such thing, but depresses that part of the narrative to the level of back-fence gossip. In his treatment of his hero's adversaries, the poet, in common with the troubadours of his day, fumbles badly, for he makes the Cid so immeasurably superior that he takes the punch out of the conflict. He creates no Hector for his Achilles. He reduces Count García Ordóñez to a mere ill-tempered grumbler who mumbles in his beard such snide remarks as: "It seems to me that hardly a man can be left alive in the land of the Moors, the Campeador

does so what he wills with them!" Neither is
there a genuine conflict with the King, who is
almost too readily bribed out of his fit of peevish-
ness. And the Moors themselves, even the great
Yusuf, are so many toy soldiers, to be toppled
over at a breath. What remains, then? Well,
the poet is singing a hymn of praise, and singing
it magnificently. That is his whole purpose.

Who can doubt his success? What else did
old Homer do? The comparison is not alto-
gether bizarre, for Homer's gallery of intensely
human heroes contains few more engaging than
Ruy Díaz and his loyal crew. The Cid's never-
failing optimism, his belief in his star (he was,
indeed, "born in a happy hour"), his generosity
above all, make him the most charming of men.
I don't mean his openhandedness with the spoils
of battle, which was plain common sense, but
his generosity of spirit. He recognizes, instantly
and wholeheartedly, any merit in his men. When
Minaya Alvar Fáñez returns from his raid along
the Henares and brings into camp a prodigious
amount of plunder, how could he resist the Cid's
greeting: "Is it you, Alvar Fáñez, my stout lance?
Where I send you, there would I expect such
deeds!" Or, when Minaya's horse is killed in
battle and the Cid gets him another from a Moor
he has slain, and shouts: "Mount, Minaya, my
right arm! I have need of you this day!" Or,
when Minaya returns from his ticklish but suc-
cessful embassy to King Alfonso and the Cid
cries: "May your days be many, Minaya! You
are a better man than I!"

The Cid's charm pervades the whole Poem and drenches it in happy sunlight. When King Yusuf comes "from beyond the sea" and pitches his camp under the walls of Valencia, the Cid's greatest joy is that his wife and daughters are there to see him "earn his bread," as he puts it. He seats his wife high in the citadel, where she can watch him at work, and says: "Ah, how my heart swells with pride to have you here to see me!" After he has put the Moors to flight with great slaughter, as he invariably does, like a good bullfighter he presents the spoils of victory to his wife and daughters in a typical *brindis:* "I salute you, ladies, and offer you these great spoils. While you held Valencia I won the field. . . . Pray God to vouchsafe me a few more years of life, and your honor will be great and men will come to kiss your hands!"

My Cid is a gracious hero.

Every student of Spanish letters must feel, as I do, a profound gratitude to Ramón Menéndez Pidal, whose critical edition of *The Poem of the Cid* has made this translation possible. My debt to him is great, but I have a more personal debt to acknowledge, to my dear old friend and teacher, Rudolph Schevill, who first opened my eyes to the beauties of ancient Spain. To his warm memory I dedicate this work of love.

LESLEY BYRD SIMPSON

REFERENCES

Ramón Menéndez Pidal, *Cantar de Mío Cid: Texto, Gramática, y Vocabulario.* 3 vols. (Madrid, 1908–1911.)

——, *La España del Cid.* 2 vols. (Madrid, 1929.)

——, *The Cid and His Spain.* Translated by H. Sutherland. (London, 1934.)

Gerald Brenan, *The Literature of the Spanish People,* Chapter III. (Cambridge, 1951.)

John Ormsby, *The Poem of the Cid. A Translation from the Spanish.* (London, 1879.)

Selden Rose and Leonard Bacon, *The Lay of the Cid.* (Berkeley, 1919.)

Archer M. Huntington (Trans.), *El Cid Campeador, Poem of the Cid.* (New York, 1942.)

CONTENTS

CHARACTERS OF THE POEM

I. The Party of the Cid

RUY (RODRIGO) DÍAZ. The Cid Campeador (Arabic *El Seid*, "the lord"), or "My Cid," as the poet prefers to call him. (*Campeador* is of uncertain etymology, but is generally taken to mean "challenger" or "battler.") Lord of the small fief of Bivar, to the north of Burgos.

DOÑA XIMENA. The Cid's "honest wife."

DOÑA ELVIRA AND DOÑA SOL. The Cid's daughters, "white as the sun."

ALVAR ALVAREZ. A vassal of the Cid.

ABENGALBÓN. Moorish castellan of Molina and the Cid's "good friend."

BABIECA "THE SWIFT." The Cid's famous horse, not the least important member of his household.

COLADA "THE PRECIOUS" AND TIZÓN. The Cid's swords, both personalities in their own right.

DIEGO TÉLLEZ. A vassal of Minaya Alvar Fáñez who receives the Cid's daughters after their rescue by Félix Muñoz.

FÉLIX MUÑOZ. A nephew of the Cid.

GALINDO GARCÍA. "He of Aragón" and "a brave lance."

JEROME. The "good Christian" from the east (i.e., France) who joins the Cid "to slay a few Moors." The Cid makes him Bishop of Valencia.

MAL ANDA. A man of law who represents the Cid at the trial of the Princes of Carrión.

MARTÍN ANTOLÍNEZ. "The noble son of Burgos" and one of the Cid's chief lieutenants. He manages the business of the swindling of the Jews; challenges Diego González, one of the Princes of Carrión.

MARTÍN MUÑOZ. A vassal of the Cid, "born under a lucky star."

MINAYA ALVAR FÁÑEZ. The Cid's chief lieutenant, counselor, and constant companion.

PEDRO BERMÚDEZ. The impetuous "Mute Pedro" and most lovable of the Cid's men. Challenger of Fernando González, Prince of Carrión and brother of Diego.

MUÑO GUSTIOZ. The Cid's "noble vassal." Challenger of Asur González of Carrión.

ABBOT DON SANCHO. Abbot of the monastery of San Pedro de Cardeña, where Doña Ximena and her daughters are sheltered during the Cid's exile.

II. The Party of Carrión

THE BENI-GÓMEZ ("sons of Gómez"). The large and important noble clan of León to which all the party of Carrión belongs.

GARCÍA ORDÓÑEZ. Count of Nájera and lord of

Grañón, the Cid's never-resting enemy whose beard the Cid plucks at the battle of Cabra. Leader of the Leonese nobles. Also known as "El Crespo de Grañón," which is to say, "the curly-haired one of Grañón."

GONZALO ANSÚREZ. Count of Carrión and father of Asur, Diego, and Fernando González.

ASUR GONZÁLEZ. The only one of the hated clan for whom the poet grudgingly has a good word, allowing that he is "a valorous man and strong," although earlier dismissing him as "quarrelsome and loose of tongue, and otherwise of little worth."

DIEGO AND FERNANDO GONZÁLEZ. The distressing Princes (*Infantes*) of Carrión, the villains of the piece.

GÓMEZ PELÁEZ.

PEDRO ANSÚREZ.

III. Judges of the King's Court at the Trial of the Princes of Carrión

ALFONSO. King of León and Castile.

COUNT ENRIQUE.

COUNT RAMÓN.

COUNT FRUELA.

COUNT BIRBÓN.

IV. Moorish Antagonists of the Cid

KING FÁRIZ.

KING GALVE.

KING BÚCAR. The "king from beyond the sea" who loses his life and Tizón at the same time, when the Cid splits him from the helmet to the waist.

KING YUSUF.

V. Other Characters

RAMÓN BERENGUER. Count of Barcelona, "a boastful man who speaks with vanity." At his misguided encounter with the Cid in the "piny wood of Tévar," in which he loses Colada "the precious" and is taken prisoner, he puts on his famous hunger strike, but, when he does eat, "God, how he enjoys it!"

RAQUEL AND VIDAS. Overtrustful moneylenders of Burgos, swindled by the Cid and Martín Antolínez.

CANTO

I

THE EXILE

M Y CID TURNED HIS HEAD AND stopped and gazed with streaming eyes. He beheld the open doors, the postern gates unbolted, and vacant the perches where once his skins and mantles hung, and his molting hawks were wont to rest.

My Cid sighed, for his heart was heavy.

My Cid spoke, well and measuredly:

"Blessed be the Lord Our God, Our Father who art on high! See now what my wicked enemies have wrought!"

Now they onward spurred, now dropped their reins. As they sallied forth from Bivar they beheld a bird of happy augury, and as they drew nigh to Burgos, one of evil omen! But My Cid shrugged his shoulders and shook his head.

"Rejoice with me, O Alvar Fáñez!" he cried. "We are cast out of our land! But we shall return, with honor, to Castile!"

Into Burgos rode My Cid, sixty lances in his company, and men and women ran out to see him. The citizens of Burgos, sorely weeping, stood at their windows, and each one made the same lament:

"God, what a worthy vassal, had he but a worthy lord!"

Gladly would they have sheltered him, but

none dared, so fearful they of the great wrath of Don Alfonso the King, for his edict had come that day to Burgos, well guarded and strongly sealed with the royal seal, commanding that none give shelter to My Cid Ruy Díaz, and that he who did so would surely lose his goods, his eyes besides, his body even, and his soul! All Christian people with grief were stricken; all fled the presence of My Cid and no one dared bespeak him. To his lodging rode the Campeador, but its door was locked in fear of King Alfonso and only by force could he have opened it. The men of My Cid shouted, but those within refused to answer. My Cid spurred forward and gave the door a mighty kick, but the door, well barred, held fast. Then up there came a little girl of nine and stood before him.

"O Campeador," cried she, "who in a happy hour girded on your sword, last night the King's edict came, well guarded and strongly sealed, forbidding us to help you. So we dare not open our doors to you for any price, nor yet give you shelter, for we should lose our goods and houses, our eyes besides. O Cid, nothing would you gain by our destruction, and may Our Lord God look after you with all His holy strength!"

Thus spoke the little girl and went back to her house.

Now did My Cid perceive he might expect no mercy from the King. So he left the door and spurred through Burgos to St. Mary's Church, and there alighted and fell upon his knees and prayed from his heart. His prayer finished, he mounted again and rode out St. Mary's Gate across the Arlanzón, and there upon a sandy spot, not far from Burgos, he pitched his tent and loosed his horse.

Thus My Cid, he who in a happy hour girded on his sword, seeing that no one would receive him, made his camp upon the sand, his goodly company about him. My Cid camped as in a wilderness, for it was forbidden him to buy his provender in the town of Burgos, and none dared sell him the smallest morsel that could be bought for money. But Martín Antolínez, that sturdy son of Burgos, got bread and wine for My Cid and his men. He bought it not, but gave of his own and supplied them well. My Cid, the excellent Campeador, was pleased with him, as were all his men.

Then up spoke Martín Antolínez. Hear now what he said:

"O Campeador, born in a happy hour, let us tarry here tonight, but tomorrow let us leave, for I shall be denounced for having served you, and the wrath of King Alfonso will be upon me. If I survive at your side, late or soon the King will want me for a friend. If he does not, well, I would not give a fig for what I leave behind."

My Cid, he who in a happy hour girded on his sword, thus made reply:

"Martín Antolínez, a sturdy lance you are! Your wages shall be doubled if I live! But now my gold is spent and all my silver. Well you know I have not wherewith to pay my company. Since I may not have it for the asking, I will take it. With your help I will make two coffers, which we will fill with sand to make them heavy and cover them with tooled leather, the leather red, the nails well gilded. Go then speedily to Raquel and Vidas and tell them this: that it is forbidden me to buy in Burgos, for the King has banished me; that I cannot bring my treasure with me, for it is heavy; and that I wish to pawn it at its just value. Let them bear it away by night, lest some Christian see it. And may Our Lord God and all His saints be judges of me, for what I do, I do because I must and can do no other."

Martín Antolínez rode swiftly through Burgos to the citadel and there asked urgently for Raquel and Vidas. These two were counting up their gains when Martín Antolínez, the prudent one, entered.

"Where are you, Raquel and Vidas, my dear friends?" cried he. "I would have a private word with you."

The three withdrew.

"And now, Raquel and Vidas," said Don Martín, "give me your solemn word that neither to Christian nor to Moor will you betray me, and I shall make you rich forever and you will never be in want again. Know, then, that when the Campeador went to collect the tribute he seized treasure in vast amount and kept for himself whatever was of value, and for this he was denounced. He has two coffers filled with gold fine-wrought. The King has banished him, as well you know, and he has abandoned his estates, his palaces and houses. He cannot bring the coffers with him, for he would be discovered. So the Campeador will leave them in your hands and you will lend him a just sum for them. Take the coffers and put them safely by, and give me your solemn word that in all the coming year you will not open them."

Raquel and Vidas communed together:

"We stand to make a profit in this business. Well we know he brought a great treasure back from Moorish lands. Ah, he sleeps not quietly who guards his money! Let us take these coffers, then, and put them safely by where they will not be found."

"But tell us now," they said to Don Martín, "what will My Cid be pleased to get for them and what usury will he pay?"

Martín Antolínez, like the prudent man he was, thus made reply:

"My Cid will accept what is just. Little will he ask if his treasure is safe. From all parts the disinherited are coming to join him and he will need six hundred marks to pay them."

"That we will give him gladly," said Raquel and Vidas.

"But night is coming on and My Cid is in great haste," said Don Martín. "We would have the money now."

"That is not the way that we do business," they replied. "We take first and give afterward."

"Agreed!" said Martín Antolínez. "Come you both with me to the illustrious Campeador and we will help you, as is right, to bear away the coffers and put them safely by where neither

Moor nor Christian shall know their resting place."

"Good!" said Raquel and Vidas. "Do you bring the coffers here and you shall have your six hundred marks."

Martín Antolínez quickly mounts, with him Raquel and Vidas, now happy and content. They cross not by the bridge, but ford the river, lest they be seen by those of Burgos.

Behold them now at the tent of the famous Campeador. They enter and kiss his hands, and My Cid smiles and speaks to them:

"Ha, Raquel and Vidas, so you have not forgotten me, although the King no longer loves me and has banished me from the land! I will share my wealth with you, I think, and so long as you both shall live you will never be in want again."

Raquel and Vidas kiss the hands of My Cid.

Martín Antolínez draws up the contract: that they will give My Cid six hundred marks for the two coffers, which they agree to keep until the year is past; that they take oath that if they open them in all that while they will be forsworn and My Cid will give them not a cursed penny for their profit.

"Take the coffers quickly now," said Martín Antolínez. "Take them, Raquel and Vidas, and put them safely by. I will go with you and bring the money, for My Cid must be off before cock-crow."

Ah, you should have seen their joy when they tried to lift the coffers! They cannot get them upon their backs, although they are strong men both! Raquel and Vidas are happy men, for they will be rich so long as they both shall live!

Raquel then kissed the hands of My Cid and said:

"O Campeador, who in a happy hour girded on your sword, you are departing from Castile and will be among foreign people. Such is your good fortune that your gains will be great. O Cid, I kiss your hands and beg you to send me a vermilion skin, Moorish and beautiful."

"That I shall do," replied My Cid. "It is granted you forthwith. I will bring it you from yonder, or, if I fail to do so, you may take its value from the coffers."

Raquel and Vidas then took up the coffers and bore them off to Burgos. They entered their lodging very quietly, spread a carpet upon the floor and over it a sheet of white linen. Don Martín then counted out three hundred silver marks, although he weighed them not. Three hundred more in gold they gave him, and Don Martín loaded the money upon the backs of his five squires. Which done, hear now what he said:

"Raquel and Vidas, the coffers are in your hands. Surely I who got them for you deserve a present."

Raquel and Vidas withdrew apart and said:

"Let us reward him well for bringing us this business."

"Martín Antolínez," they said to him, "famed son of Burgos, well have you earned a present!

Take now this rich skin and this good cloth and with them make yourself doublet and hose. Take these thirty marks besides—you well deserve them. This is only just, for you were the mediator of our contract."

Don Martín thanked them and took the money, then bade them farewell and rode forth from Burgos across the Arlanzón and came to the tent of him who in a happy hour was born. My Cid received him with open arms.

"Martín Antolínez, my faithful vassal!" he cried. "You have returned! May I see the day when I can reward you!"

"Good news, O Campeador!" said Martín Antolínez. "Good news! You have your six hundred marks and I my thirty! Order your tent struck and let us go in haste, and let cockcrow find us in San Pedro de Cardeña, where we shall see your noble wife. But make our stay there brief and let us leave the kingdom, as needs must, for our time grows short."

He spoke and the tent was struck, and My Cid and his men mounted in all haste. My Cid turned his horse's head toward St. Mary's Church and raised his right hand and crossed himself, praying:

"I thank Thee, O God, Lord of heaven and earth! O glorious St. Mary, lend me Thy strength! Now must I depart from Castile, for the King loves me not, and I know not whether I shall return in all the days of my life. Help me, Glorious One, in my exile! Help and succor me both day and night! If Thou do so, and fortune

favor me, good and beautiful gifts shall I bring
Thee for thy altar. And I further promise I shall
have a thousand masses sung in praise of Thee."

The illustrious one thus took his leave, his heart
heavy and his spirit low, and his men mounted
and spurred on. Then up spoke Martín Antolínez,
that loyal son of Burgos:

"I wish to see my wife unhurriedly and leave
instructions with my people. And if the King
seize my estate, well, it matters not. I shall be
with you again before the break of day."

Martín Antolínez then turned back to Burgos
and My Cid spurred on toward San Pedro de
Cardeña with his knights who gladly served him.

The cocks were loudly crowing and day was
breaking when the good Campeador came to San
Pedro. Abbot Don Sancho, that excellent Chris-
tian, was saying matins, and Doña Ximena, with
her the five noble ladies of her household, was
thus praying to St. Peter and Our Lord:

"O Thou who rulest all, help Thou My Cid
the Campeador!"

My Cid knocks. The news travels fast! God,
how happy is Abbot Don Sancho! All run to the
courtyard with lamps and torches to welcome
him who in a happy hour was born.

"Thank God that you have come!" cried Ab-
bot Don Sancho. "O Cid, this is your house!"

"I thank you, Sir Abbot," answered My Cid.
"I am in your debt; but I shall tarry only to
feed myself and men, for I must leave the
country. Take these fifty marks, which I shall

double if I live, for I would put the monastery
to no pennyworth of expense. Receive besides
these hundred marks for the service of Doña
Ximena and her daughters and ladies-in-waiting
this year. Cherish these daughters of mine, Abbot
Don Sancho! I commend them to you. Serve
them and my wife with all loving-kindness, and
if this sum should not suffice, let them lack for
nothing, I beseech you. For each mark you spend
in their behalf four will I give the monastery."

The Abbot willingly agreed.

And now behold Doña Ximena who comes to
My Cid, her daughters in the arms of their
nurses. Doña Ximena kneels before the Cam-
peador, sorely weeping, and would kiss his hands.

"O Campeador," she cried, "born in a happy
hour, grant me now this boon! You are banished
from the land by the work of wicked men. A
boon, My Cid of the noble beard! Behold me
here before you with your daughters, babies still,
few in days, and these my ladies who serve me.
You are leaving me and we must part in life.
For St. Mary's love tell us what we must do!"

He of the noble beard held out his hands to
his daughters and pressed them to his heart, for
he loved them much. He wept and sighed heavily,
saying:

"Ah, Doña Ximena, my noble wife, I love you
as I love my soul! We must part in life: I go and
you remain. May it please God and St. Mary
that I may yet give these my daughters in mar-
riage with my own hands and that I have the
good fortune to live yet a little while in which
to serve you, my honest wife!"

In San Pedro de Cardeña a great feast is spread for the Campeador and the bells ring out.

In Castile the banishment of My Cid the Campeador is everywhere proclaimed, and some abandon their houses, others their estates, to join him. That very day a hundred and fifteen knights gather at the bridge of the Arlanzón and ask where My Cid the Campeador may be. Martín Antolínez meets them there and they set out for San Pedro de Cardeña, where he is who in a happy hour was born.

My Cid heard that his company had increased, and mounted and went forth to meet them. When he saw them he smiled again, and all came up to kiss his hands. My Cid spoke joyfully:

"I pray God Our Heavenly Father that, before I die, I may reward you who have left your houses and estates for me! What you lose thereby you shall regain twofold!"

My Cid was happy to see his company increase, and all shared his happiness.

Know you now that six days of his term have passed and three remain, no more. The King has commanded that My Cid be watched and that if he be taken in the land after his term he escape not for gold or silver.

The day is done and night is falling. My Cid gathers his knights about him and speaks to them:

"Listen, my barons, and be not afflicted by what you shall hear. I have little money, but of what there is you shall have your share. Hear now what you must do. In the morning at cockcrow you will have your horses saddled. The good

Abbot will ring for matins at St. Peter's and say
the Mass of the Holy Trinity, and after Mass
we shall ride, for the end of my term approaches
and we have yet a long way to go."

As My Cid has commanded, so will they do.
The night ends and day breaks, and at the second
cockcrow they have their horses saddled.

The bells for matins are loudly rung, and My
Cid and his wife hear Mass. Doña Ximena casts
herself down upon the altar steps and thus prays
Our Lord to shield My Cid the Campeador from
all evil:

"Glorious Lord, Our Father who art in heaven,
Creator of heaven and earth, the sea, the stars and
the moon, and the sun which warms us, made
flesh in our Mother Mary, born in Bethlehem
according to Thy will, where the shepherds mag-
nified and praised Thee, where the three Kings of
Araby came to adore Thee, Melchior, Gaspar,
and Balthasar, and brought Thee a glad offering
of gold and myrrh and frankincense;

"Thou who didst save Jonah when he fell into
the sea, and Daniel from the lions in their noisome
den, and in Rome didst save St. Sebastian, and
Susanna from the lying slanderer;

"Thou, O Spiritual Father, who didst wander
over the earth for two-and-thirty years working
Thy renowned miracles, making wine of water
and bread of stones, and bringing Lazarus back to
life by the strength of Thy will;

"Thou who didst allow the Jews to seize Thee
on Mt. Calvary and nail Thee to the Cross at

Golgotha, between two thieves, the one now in Paradise, the other who entered not;

"Thou who, whilst Thou wert on the Cross, didst yet another miracle, for Longinus, a blind man who had never seen anything at all, but who wet his hands in Thy blood which was dripping from the shaft of the lance thrust in Thy side, and with it touched his face, and straightway saw and believed in Thee who thus didst cure him;

"Thou who didst come to life again in the tomb and descend into hell, as was Thy will;

"Thou who didst break open the doors and release the Holy Fathers;

"Thou who art King of Kings and Father of all;

"I adore Thee and believe in Thee with all my heart, and I beg St. Peter to help me pray God to shield My Cid the Campeador from harm and, though we now must part, to grant that we meet again in life!"

The prayer was done, the Mass said, and all left the church ready to mount. My Cid embraced Doña Ximena and she kissed his hands, weeping and knowing not what to do. He gazed upon his daughters and said:

"To God Our Father I now commend you. Now we must part and God knows when we shall meet again!"

Ah, such sorrow was never seen! They parted as the nail is parted from the flesh.

My Cid mounted with his vassals, but turned

his head and tarried. Then up spoke Minaya Alvar Fáñez and wisely said:

"O Cid, whose mother bore you in a happy hour, where is your strength? We must ride and leave this idle talk. All these troubles will yet turn to pleasures. God who gave us life will give us counsel."

But My Cid tarried yet a while, pleading with Abbot Don Sancho to protect Doña Ximena and her children, and promised him a rich reward. Don Sancho then turned back and Alvar Fáñez said to him:

"Should more men come to join us, Abbot, have them follow us in all haste, and in town or wilderness they will find us."

They give their horses their heads and are on their way, for the hour to leave the kingdom is at hand.

My Cid stopped at Espinazo de Can, where many men joined him that night, coming from all parts.

Banished is My Cid, the loyal one!

The next day in the morning they were on the road again, on their left San Esteban, that good city. My Cid passed Alcubilla, which is the limit of Castile, and left by the Quinea road. He crossed the Duero at Navapalos and ended his day's journey at Figueruela. And all along the way men came from every part to join him.

Night fell and My Cid lay down. Sweet slumber overcame him and soundly did he sleep. And the Angel Gabriel appeared to him in a dream and said·

"Ride, O Cid, my good Campeador, for never did knight ride so luckily! Things will go well with you so long as you shall live!"

My Cid awoke and crossed himself. Which done, he commended himself to God, well pleased with his dream.

The next morning they mount again, for, know you, it is the last day of his term. They rest at Sierra de Miedes, on their right the towers of Atienza held by the Moors. While it is still day and the sun has not yet set, My Cid commands his men to parade. Leaving out the valiant men of his foot, he counts three hundred lances, all with their pennants.

"In the morning you will feed your horses," said he, "and God save you! Let him who wishes, eat; if not, let him mount. We shall cross the mountains, high and rugged, and this night we shall be beyond the land of King Alfonso. And then let him who seeks us find us!"

In the night they cross the mountains. Dawn comes and they descend the other side. In the midst of a wonderful great wood My Cid calls a halt to feed the horses and tell his men they will march again that night. And they, good vassals that they are, willingly obey him. Whatever their lord commands, that will they do. They ride again before nightfall and march by night, lest they be seen. They give themselves no rest and, near the town of Castejón on the Henares, My Cid sets an ambush. He lay in ambush all that night and Alvar Fáñez counseled him, saying:

"O Cid, who in a happy hour girded on your

sword, since we plan to take Castejón by surprise, do you remain in the rear with a hundred men of our company, while I take two hundred and ride on ahead. With God's help and your good luck we shall take much booty."

"Well spoken, Alvar Fáñez!" replied My Cid the Campeador. "Do you lead the van with two hundred, and let Alvar Alvarez go with you, and Alvar Salvadórez, and Galindo García, a brave lance, good barons all! Strike boldly, lest you lose your spoils through fear. Let the van advance downsteam from Hita past Guadalajara, as far as Alcalá. Make sure of your prizes and lose nothing from fear of the Moors. I with my hundred, flanked by Castejón, will hold the rear. If you have trouble send me word and all Spain will talk of the help I give you!"

The men of the van are told off, and those who will remain in the rear. Now dawn is breaking and morning is at hand. The sun shines forth. God, how beautiful it is!

The people of Castejón arise and open their gates and go forth to tend their fields. All have now left, their gates are wide, and few remain in Castejón. The people are scattered without.

The Campeador then leaves his ambush and makes for the gate. The guards see him coming and abandon it in fear. My Cid Ruy Díaz, bare sword in hand, then attacks and slays some fifteen Moors who oppose him. He takes Castejón and all its gold and silver. His knights bring up the booty and leave it with My Cid. They value it not at all.

Behold now the two hundred of the van and three, how they boldly ride and sack the countryside. Minaya's standard reaches Alcalá. They bring their booty up the Henares by Guadalajara. Great are the spoils: many flocks of sheep and herds of cattle, and clothing and other riches. Minaya's standard holds firm and none dares attack his rear. Laden with spoils the company returns. Behold them once again in Castejón, where the Campeador awaits them. My Cid leaves the castle to its guard and marches forth with all his men. He greets Minaya, embracing him:

"Is it you, Alvar Fáñez, my stout lance? Where I send you there would I expect such deeds! Let us heap together all our spoils and of all our gains I will give you the fifth part, Minaya, if you will accept it."

"Much do I thank you, illustrious Campeador!" replied Alvar Fáñez. "The Castilian Alfonso himself would be happy to have this fifth you offer me! But I yield it to you; you owe me nothing. Before God on high I vow that until I am sated with fighting Moors on the field of battle, mounted on my good horse, thrusting with my lance and striking with my sword, their blood dripping from my elbow down, in the presence of My Cid Ruy Díaz, the renowned Battler, I shall take from you not a cursed penny! When with my help you shall have won something of worth, very well, but the rest, lo, it is yours!"

The spoils are heaped up. My Cid, he who in a happy hour girded on his sword, thinks that Alfonso's men may come and seek him out, so he commands that all the booty be divided and the umpires verify what each is to receive. His knights get a goodly share, each a hundred marks, the foot half as much, and My Cid is given all his fifth. But he cannot sell it here, nor yet give it as a present; nor does he wish to keep the captives, men and women, in his company. He speaks with those of Castejón and sends word also to Hita and Guadalajara. However great the price they pay for his fifth, they will profit greatly. They offer three thousand marks and after three days pay him faithfully.

My Cid thinks they cannot remain in the castle and his men agree with him. They can, indeed, defend it, but hold it they cannot, for lack of water.

"Now that the Moors are pacified," said he, "and the treaty is signed, King Alfonso may seek us out with all his forces. Hear me now, my men, and hear me, Minaya, and be not offended by what I say. I wish to abandon Castejón, for King Alfonso is close by and may attack us. But I will not destroy the castle. I will set free two hundred of these Moors, lest they speak ill of me for what I have seized of theirs. All of you have now your share of the booty and none is left unpaid. We will depart in the morning, for I will not fight my lord King Alfonso."

All approve the words of My Cid. All, now rich, abandon the castle they have taken, and the Moors, men and women, bless Him. They march up the Henares as far as they may go, beyond Alcarria and the Caves of Anguita, and across the river and well into the Plain of Taranz.

My Cid encamps between Ariza and Cetina. In all parts, wherever he goes, he amasses great booty. The Moors know not his plan. The next day My Cid, he of Bivar, moves on beyond Alhama and La Hoz, Briviesca also, and Ateca, and halts at Alcocer, on a round hill, high and strong. Near by runs the Jalón, so that water cannot be denied him.

My Cid, Don Rodrigo, plans to take Alcocer!

He makes his camp upon the hill, some of his tents upon the heights, others on the river. The good Campeador, he who in a happy hour girded on his sword, puts all his men to work digging a trench, so that neither by day nor by night can they be surprised, and so that all the world may know here dwells My Cid!

It is quickly noised throughout the land that My Cid has left Christendom and is now settled among the Moors, who hardly dare to work their fields. My Cid rejoices, as do all his men, for the castle of Alcocer will soon pay them tribute.

Those of Alcocer do pay tribute to My Cid, and those of Ateca as well, and the town of Terrer; but those of Calatayud, know you, like it not at all.

Fifteen full weeks My Cid rested there, and when he saw that Alcocer would not yield he planned a stratagem and put it promptly into effect. Striking all his tents save one, he marched off down the Jalón, pennants flying, clad in their coats of mail, swords buckled on—all this to deceive those of Alcocer. They saw him go and, God, how pleased they were!

"The Cid's provisions have failed him," they said. "He had not time to strike his tents and has left one standing. My Cid is marching off to escape disaster! Let us attack him now and win great booty, before those of Terrer capture him, for if they do they will leave nothing for us. He shall pay us doubly for the tribute he has taken!"

They sally forth from Alcocer with wonderful speed. My Cid sees them and pretends to fly. Down the Jalón he spurs with his men.

"There go our spoils!" shout those of Alcocer, and young and old run out, in their mouths the taste of booty, leaving their open gates unguarded.

The good Campeador turns his head and sees a wide space between the Moors and the castle. He commands that his standard be reversed and his men spur back.

"At them, my knights!" he cried. "Strike fearlessly! With the help of God we shall win this day!"

In the midst of the plain the battle is joined. God, what a happy morning! My Cid and Alvar Fáñez spur on ahead, for they have good mounts, and cut the Moors off from the castle. The vassals of My Cid strike without pity and in a brief space slay three hundred Moors. Now his men who have been in ambush set up a great shout and run out with bared swords. They halt at the gate, but soon the rest join them and the victory is theirs.

——— Thus by a stratagem did the Cid win Alcocer.

Pedro Bermúdez, who bore the standard,

climbed up and planted it in the highest place. Then spoke My Cid, born in a happy hour:

"Thanks be to God in heaven and to all His saints! We now have better quarters for our horses and their riders! Hear me now, Alvar Fáñez and all my knights. We have won great spoils in this castle. We have slain many Moors and I see few alive. The captives, men and women, cannot be sold, and we would gain nothing by beheading them. Let us bring them back to the castle, then, now that we are the masters, and we can lodge in their houses and use them in our service."

My Cid is now in Alcocer, with all his booty, and sends for the tent he had left standing.

Those of Ateca like it not at all, nor do those of Terrer, and those of Calatayud, know you, take it very hard. They send word to King Mutamin of Valencia, that a certain Cid, Ruy Díaz de Bivar, who was banished by King Alfonso, is encamped in a strong place near Alcocer and by a stratagem has taken the castle.

"If you come not to our aid," they said, "you will lose Ateca and Terrer, Calatayud besides, which cannot escape. All will be lost in the valley of the Jalón, as well as in that of the Jiloca beyond."

King Mutamin heard and was dismayed. Said he:

"I have three Moorish kings here with me. Do two of you proceed thither without delay, with three thousand men, well armed. With the help

SPAIN

in the time of the Cid,
late eleventh century.

After Menéndez Pidal.

· Fritz L Kramer – 1957·

of those of the frontier take him alive and bring
him before me. He shall pay for invading my
lands!"

The three thousand mount and are on their
way. By nightfall they are at Segorbe. The next
morning they ride on and that evening come to
Celfa. They send word to those of the frontier,
who quickly gather from every part. They leave
Celfa del Canal, as it is called, and march the
whole day without rest, and by nightfall are at
Calatayud. They send criers throughout the land
and a great multitude assembles about the two
kings, Fáriz and Galve. They plan to besiege My
Cid in Alcocer.

They pitch their tents and make their camp.
Their forces grow and they now have many men.
They post sentries day and night, all fully armed.
Many are the sentries, great is the host! They
cut off the water of My Cid and his men. My
Cid's companies wish to go forth and give battle,
but he who in a happy hour was born forbids it.
He is besieged for three full weeks. At the end
of the third and as the fourth is beginning My
Cid calls his men to council and says:

"Our water has been cut off and our provi-
sions are failing. They will not allow us to leave
by night and they are too strong for us to fight.
Tell me now, my barons, what is your pleas-
ure?"

Then up spoke Minaya, that excellent knight,
and said:

"We are far from our noble Castile and can
win our bread only by fighting the Moors. We

number six hundred, perhaps a few more. In God's name let us attack them tomorrow! This only let us do!"

"You speak to my liking, Minaya!" said the Campeador. "You honor yourself thereby, as I expected of you."

My Cid commands that all the Moors, men and women, be expelled from Alcocer, lest they betray his plan. All that day and all that night the Cid's men arm themselves, and in the morning, just at sunrise, My Cid and his men are ready. My Cid speaks. Hear now what he says:

"We will ride forth and let none remain save two men to hold the gate, and if we die in the field they may have their castle! If we win we shall be the richer! Do you, Pedro Bermúdez, bear my standard. You are a stout man and will guard it faithfully, but do not advance with it until I so order."

Bermúdez takes the standard and kisses My Cid's hands. The gate is opened and they dash forth. The Moorish sentries see them coming and speedily give the alarm. How quickly do the Moors don their armor! At the roll of their drums the very earth trembles! Ah, you should have seen them take their arms and form their lines! They have two royal standards, and the pennants mingled amongst them, who can count them? The Moorish lines advance to attack My Cid.

"Stand your ground, my men!" cries he. "Let no man move until I give the word!"

But Pedro Bermúdez cannot contain himself,

and with the standard in his hand he spurs forward, shouting:

"Now God be with you, loyal Cid the Campeador! I shall bear your standard into the thick of their lines. Let us now see whether your vassals will rally round it!"

"Stop, for the love of God!" cried My Cid.

"Nothing in the world can stop me!" replied Bermúdez.

He spurs his horse and charges into the lines. The Moors await him to seize the standard. They deal him heavy blows, but cannot pierce his armor.

"Help him, if you love me!" cried My Cid.

His men embrace their shields and lower their lances, pennants flying. They lean forward in their saddles and attack with strong hearts. With great shouts he who in a happy hour was born urges them on:

"Strike, my knights, in the name of God! I am Ruy Díaz the Cid, the Campeador of Bivar!"

All charge the line where Pedro Bermúdez is, three hundred lances with their pennants! Each one slays his Moor, and upon their return they slay as many more!

Ah, you should have seen all those lances striking, piercing and bursting shields and coats of mail, all those white pennants now red with blood, all those horses running riderless! The Moors invoke Mohammed, the Christians St. James, and in a little while a thousand and three hundred Moors lie dead upon the field!

Ah, how well does My Cid Ruy Díaz the good fighter do battle from his gilded saddle! And Minaya Alvar Fáñez, who commanded at Zorita! And Martín Antolínez, that noble son of Burgos! And Muño Gustioz, that servant of the Cid! And Martín Muñoz, who commanded at Monte Mayor! And Alvar Alvarez! And Alvar Salvadórez! And Galindo García, the good Aragonese! And Félix Muñoz, that nephew of the Campeador! And so with all the rest, all charge to the rescue of My Cid and his standard.

The horse of Minaya Alvar Fáñez is killed, but well is he succored by the Christian squadrons. His lance is broken, but he grasps his sword and smites mightily, now on foot. My Cid Ruy Díaz the Castilian sees his plight and attacks a Moorish knight, well mounted, and strikes him a blow that cleaves him through the middle and drops him to the ground. The Moor's horse he gives to Minaya, shouting:

"Mount, Minaya, my right arm! I have need of you this day! The Moors stand fast and hold the field. Let us finish them!"

Minaya mounts, sword in hand. He fights valiantly and destroys all he meets. My Cid Ruy Díaz, he who in a happy hour was born, thrusts thrice at King Fáriz. Twice he misses, but at the third thrust he strikes home and the blood gushes forth. The Moor turns tail and flies the field. With that single blow the Moorish host is vanquished.

Martín Antolínez aims a blow at King Galve

which cuts the rubies from his helmet and touches his flesh. The Moor tarries not for a second blow, of this you may be sure!

King Fáriz and King Galve are defeated. What a day for the Christians! The Moors are flying in all directions and the men of My Cid pursue them. King Fáriz takes refuge in Terrer, but King Galve is not admitted, and he gallops full speed to Calatayud, pursued the whole distance by the Campeador.

The horse of Minaya Alvar Fáñez serves him well. He slays thirty-four of those Moors! His blade is sharp and his arm is all bloody and dripping from the elbow down.

"Now I am quit!" he cries. "The good news will reach Castile, how My Cid has won this battle!"

Many Moors lie dead about him. He strikes them as they fly and leaves few alive.

The men of him who in a happy hour was born now return. My Cid, sword in hand, is riding his good horse, his hood thrown back, his coif open. God, what a beard he has! His men approach.

"Thanks be to God on high!" he shouts. "Ours is this great victory!"

My Cid's men sack the Moorish camp, taking shields and arms and riches in profusion. They gather up the horses of the Moors and find they have five hundred and ten. And how great their joy when they learn they have lost but fifteen of their men! They have so much gold and silver

that they know not what to do with it. The
Christians all are rich with booty.

The Moors of Alcocer are brought back to
their castle and My Cid commands they be re-
warded. My Cid rejoices with all his vassals. He
has the great spoils distributed, and his fifth comes
to a hundred horses. God, how well does he pay
his vassals, foot as well as horse! He does wisely,
he who in a happy hour was born, and all his men
are well content.

good to vassals

"Hear me now, Minaya, my right arm," said
he. "Of these riches that the Creator has given
us take what you will. I wish to send you to
Castile with the news of this great battle we have
won, and for King Alfonso who banished me, a
gift of thirty horses, all saddled and bridled,
with swords hanging from their saddlebows."

still loyal to his vassal

"Gladly will I do so!" replied Minaya Alvar
Fáñez.

"And take this boot well filled with gold and
silver, and with it pay for a thousand masses at
St. Mary's of Burgos. What is left give to my
wife and daughters and have them pray for me
night and day. If I live they shall be rich!"

Minaya Alvar Fáñez is well content. Those of
his company are named and they feed their
horses. At nightfall My Cid calls his men to
council and says:

"You are going, Minaya, to Castile the noble.
You will tell our friends that with God's help we
have won this battle. When you return you will

find us here, or, if you do not, learn where we
have gone and follow us, for we must live by our
swords and lances. Otherwise, in this lean land
we could not survive and would have to go else-
where."

The land is lean indeed!

All is arranged. Minaya departs in the morn-
ing and the Campeador remains at Alcocer with
his men.

Every day the Moors of the frontier spy upon
My Cid. King Fáriz recovers from his wound
and lends them his counsel, informing them that
My Cid has made a treaty with those of Ateca
and Terrer, that city, and with those of Calata-
yud, which is the richest; that the treaty has been
signed, and that My Cid has sold the castle of
Alcocer for three thousand marks.

My Cid has sold Alcocer! How well he pays
his vassals! Horse and foot are all made rich and
not a poor man is among them. He who serves a
good master, how well paid is he!

My Cid quits the castle and the Moors, men
and women, fall to weeping.

"And are you leaving us, My Cid?" they cry.
"May our prayers go with you! We thank you,
lord, for your gift to us!"

My Cid, he of Bivar, quits Alcocer, and the
Moors, men and women, weep.

The Campeador raises his standard and sets
forth. Down the Jalón he spurs, and as he crosses
the river he reads a lucky augury in the flight of
birds. Those of Terrer are pleased at his going,

as are those of Calatayud, but those of Alcocer
are sad, so well has he rewarded them.

My Cid rides on as far as El Poyo, which is in
Monreal, high and marvelous to see, fearing no
attack, know you, from any side. First he makes
Daroca his tributary, then Molina beyond it;
third, Teruel; and finally he took Celfa del Canal.

May God bless My Cid Ruy Díaz!

Alvar Fáñez, now in Castile, presents the
thirty horses to the King, who sees them and
smiles with pleasure.

"God bless you, Minaya!" said he. "And who
sends me them?"

"My Cid Ruy Díaz, he who in a happy hour
girded on his sword! After his banishment he
took Alcocer by a stratagem. The King of Va-
lencia, hearing of it, laid siege to him and cut off
his water. But My Cid sallied forth and fought
him in the field and vanquished two Moorish
kings in battle. Great were the spoils he took,
lord! To you, noble King, he sends this gift. He
kisses your feet and hands and begs a boon of you
in the name of God."

"It is early in the day," replied the King, "to
receive, after a few short weeks, a banished man
who has lost the love of his lord. But I will
accept his gift, taken as it was from the Moors,
and I am even pleased with My Cid who won such
spoils. And as for you, Minaya, I restore to you
your honors and your lands. Come and go as you
will. You have my permission. But of My Cid I

tell you naught save this, Minaya: that all who wish to go and serve him have my leave to do so, and their goods will not be seized."

Minaya Alvar Fáñez kissed the King's hands and said:

"I thank you, O King, my natural lord, for what you have done and for what you will do hereafter, for with the help of God we shall do such deeds as will persuade you!"

"Enough of this, Minaya!" said the King. "Go now freely through Castile and rejoin My Cid and fear not."

I will tell you now of him who in a happy hour girded on his sword. That hill whereon he camped, so long as there are Moors and Christians, will be called *El Poyo del Cid*. From it he overran the country round and put the whole valley of the Martín under tribute to him. Word of his deeds came to Zaragoza and caused great anxiety among the Moors.

My Cid remained there for three weeks, no less, and when the illustrious one saw that Minaya was long in returning, he took his men and sallied forth by night, abandoning El Poyo and going beyond Teruel, and there encamped in the piny wood of Tévar. All the land through which he passed he put to the sack, and made Zaragoza his tributary.

He spent three weeks at this, and then Minaya returned from Castile, bringing in his company two hundred knights, all armed, and foot too numerous to count. When My Cid saw Minaya he spurred up and embraced him—nay, he kissed his mouth and the eyes of his face. Minaya told his tale, concealing nothing, and the Campeador smiled happily and said:

"I thank God and all His saints! While you live, Minaya, all will go well with me!"

God, how happy were the Cid's men at the return of Minaya Alvar Fáñez, for he brought them word of their brothers and cousins and the wives they had left behind! And, God, how happy was he of the noble beard to learn that Alvar Fáñez had paid for the thousand masses and seen his wife and daughters! God, how happy was he and how he rejoiced!

"May your days be many, Alvar Fáñez!" he cried. "You are a better man than I! Well did you fulfill your mission!"

He who in a happy hour was born chose forthwith two hundred knights and set out upon a night foray. He made a desert of the land of Alcañiz and sacked the countryside, and after three days he returned again to his starting place.

News of it flew throughout the land. Those of Monzón and Huesca were troubled, but those of Zaragoza were glad to pay tribute to My Cid, from whom they feared no outrage.

Laden with spoils all returned joyfully to their encampment, to the great pleasure of My Cid, and especially of Alvar Fáñez. The excellent one could not withhold his smiles.

"Hear me, my knights," said he, "and I will tell you a truth: that he who stays in one spot will see his estate diminish. Tomorrow, then, let us mount and leave this camp and be on our way."

My Cid moved on to the Pass of Olocau, and thence to Huesa and Montalbán. In this raid he spent ten days. It was soon known everywhere that it was the exile from Castile who was spoiling the countryside. The word sped and came to the ears of the Count of Barcelona, that it was My Cid Ruy Díaz who was thus wasting the land. This he took as a grave affront and was very angry. The count was a boastful man and spoke with vanity:

"My Cid, he of Bivar, is doing me great injury. While at my court he did the same, for he wounded my nephew and did no satisfaction for it. And now he is ravaging the lands of my protectorate! I have never challenged him, nor yet broken friendship with him, but now that he is attacking me I shall call him to account!"

Great are his forces, Moorish and Christian, and they assemble in haste and set out to seek My Cid, the worthy one of Bivar. Three days and three nights they march, and come upon My Cid in the piny wood of Tévar. So strong are they that they think to take him with their bare hands!

My Cid Don Rodrigo, laden with his spoils, descends from the mountains and enters into a valley, and there hears of the advance of Count Ramón. My Cid hears of it and sends him this message:

"Tell the count not to be offended by what I

do and to leave me in peace, for I have taken nothing of his."

"Not so!" replied the count. "My Cid shall pay me now for what he has done in the past! The banished one shall see who it is he comes to insult!"

The messenger returns in all haste, and now My Cid, he of Bivar, knows he must do battle.

"Ho, my knights!" he cried. "Put aside your booty and quickly arm, for Count Ramón is coming to attack us! He has a multitude of men, Moors and Christians, and we have no choice but to fight him. If we fly he will overtake us, so let us meet him here. Tighten your saddle girths, then, and don your armor. Here they come, down from the hills! But they wear hose and mount only riding saddles, badly cinched, while we wear boots and mount stout Galician saddles. A hundred of us are a match for that whole multitude! Before they come upon the plain we will charge them with lances. For every one you stick, three saddles will be emptied. And now Ramón Berenguer shall see the kind of man he has tracked this day to the piny wood of Tévar, thinking to seize his booty!"

Thus speaks My Cid and all make ready, mounting their horses and grasping their lances. The Frankish forces come down from the hills. They advance to the edge of the plain, and My Cid, born in a happy hour, orders the charge. His men attack with spirit, plying their lances, pennants flying, piercing some and unhorsing others. The Campeador wins the battle and takes prisoner Count Ramón himself. He also wins the famous sword Colada, worth more than a thousand marks!

Thus he who in a happy hour was born wins honor for his beard. He brings the count a prisoner to his tent and commands his servants to guard him, while he goes out and is joined by all his men. My Cid is pleased, for vast are his spoils. A great feast is spread for My Cid Don Rodrigo, but Count Ramón will have none of it. Food is set before him, but he scorns it and will not eat.

"I would not touch a morsel," cried he, "for all the wealth of Spain! Rather would I lose my body and my soul! To think that I was vanquished by such a rabble!"

Then up spoke My Cid. Hear now what he said:

"Eat the bread, count, and drink the wine. If you do so I will set you free. If not, never in all your days will you see Christendom again!"

"Don Rodrigo," replied the count, "eat, if it please you, and rest, but as for me I shall never eat again!"

Even after three days, while they divide the spoils, they cannot persuade the count to take a crumb of bread.

"Eat something, count," said My Cid. "Otherwise, you will never see Christendom again. But if you eat to my liking I shall set you at liberty and two of your knights as well."

When the count heard this he took heart and said:

"If you do as you say, O Cid, I shall never cease to marvel thereat so long as I shall live!"

"Then eat, count," said My Cid, "and when you have broken your fast I shall set you and two others at liberty. But of what you have lost in battle, and I have won, know you that I shall not return a cursed pennyworth, for I have need of it to pay those who have suffered with me. We earn our bread by taking it from you and the rest, until God our Father do otherwise dispose, for we are in disgrace with the King and he has cast us out."

good vassal

The count is cheered. He begs water for his hands and is gladly served. With his knights that My Cid has set at liberty the count eats and, God, how he enjoys it! He who in a happy hour was born sits beside him and says:

"If you eat not to my liking, count, here we shall remain for the rest of our days."

"I shall eat with pleasure," replied the count.

With his two knights he breakfasts well, and My Cid is pleased to see how quickly Count Ramón plies his hands.

"If it please you, My Cid," the count then said, "we are ready to depart. If you will have our horses saddled we shall ride speedily away. Never in all the days since I was made a count have I eaten so well! Its taste I never shall forget!"

Three palfreys are given them, well saddled, and good garments, and skins and mantles. Count Ramón rides between the other two, and our Castilian escorts them to the end of the camp.

"You are leaving us, count," he says, "free as a Frank! I am obliged to you for the riches you leave behind. Should you ever think to avenge yourself and seek me out again, send me word, and you will leave us more of your wealth, or you will take some of mine."

"Trouble yourself not on that account, My Cid," replied the count. "There is no danger of that! I have paid my dues for this whole year and, as for my seeking you out, it is not to be thought of!"

The count spurs away, turning his head ever and anon to look back, so fearful he lest My Cid repent, a thing which the excellent one would not do for all the wealth in the world, for never has he committed an act of perfidy.

The count departs, and he of Bivar gathers his men about him and they rejoice at the booty they have taken, marvelous and great. So rich are they that they know not what they have.

CANTO

II

THE WEDDING

AND NOW I WILL CONTINUE THE song of the exploits of My Cid, he of Bivar.

My Cid occupied the Pass of Olocau, leaving behind him Zaragoza and its lands, and the lands of Huesa and those of Montalbán. And now on the shore of the salt sea he began to wage war. The sun rises in the east, and thither went My Cid. My Cid took Jérica, Onda, and Almenara, and the lands of Burriana, he took them all. Our Lord God who is in heaven was with him, and great grew the fear of him among those of Valencia.

Those of Valencia, know you, were far from pleased, so they took counsel among themselves and decided to lay siege to him. They spent the night upon the road and at daybreak pitched their tents near Murviedro. My Cid marveled and said:

"I thank Thee, O Spiritual Father! We are in their land doing them all manner of harm, drinking their wine and eating their bread. Good reason have they to lay siege to us! If we do not fight them now this will be the end of us. Let us summon help from Jérica, Olocau, Onda, and Almenara. Let those of Burriana join us also and speedily, and we will do battle. With God's help this will bring us honor!"

By the third day all had gathered, and he who in a happy hour was born thus addressed them:

"Listen, my comrades, and may God bless you! Ever since we left our unsullied Christian land— unwillingly we did so, for we had no choice— with the help of God things have gone well with us. Those of Valencia now surround us. If we would stay firmly in their land we must teach them a lesson. When night has passed and morning comes let me find your arms and horses ready, and we shall go forth and test this army of theirs! We are exiles in a foreign land. Let us see now who earns his wages!"

Hear now what Alvar Fáñez replied:

"Campeador, let us do as you desire. Give me a hundred knights—I want no more—and do you with the rest attack them in front. Strike hard and fearlessly, and I with my hundred will take them in the rear, and with God's help, I trust, the field will be ours."

Thus spoke he and My Cid was pleased.

Morning came and they armed themselves. Each one knew his part. At the first light My Cid fell upon his adversaries, shouting:

"In the name of God and the Apostle St. James, strike them, my knights, with all your strength, for I am Ruy Díaz, the Cid, he of Bivar!"

Ah, you should have seen all those tent ropes broken, those stakes pulled up, those tent poles falling in all directions! But the Moors are many and reform their ranks. Then, from behind, Alvar Fáñez strikes, and willy-nilly they yield and fly, those who can, at full gallop. In the pursuit two Moorish kings are slain, and the chase continues to the very gates of Valencia.

Great are the spoils won by My Cid! His men loot the camp and turn back to Murviedro bearing their booty, while all the town rejoices. Conquered is Puig and the country roundabout. Those of Valencia are filled with fear and know not what to do.

The fame of My Cid, know you, goes on before him and his renown is bruited beyond the seas. My Cid is happy and so are his companions, for God was with them in their victory.

My Cid sends forth his messengers who ride by night as far as Cullera and Játiva, and farther, to Denia, that city. Along the shore My Cid ravages the lands of the Moors and takes Benicadell with all its approaches.

My Cid takes Benicadell, and those of Játiva and Cullera like it not, while the grief of Valencia is beyond measure.

Sleeping by day and marching by night, My Cid spends three years in the lands of the Moors, seizing and sacking their cities. Those of Valencia learn caution and no longer dare sally forth to meet him. He fells their orchards and does them much hurt in each of these three years, cutting off their food. Those of Valencia are troubled and know not what to do, for nowhere can they find bread. Parents cannot help their

children, nor children their parents, and friends
have no comfort for friends. Ah, my lords, it is
a bitter thing to have no bread and see your
wives and children perishing of hunger!

Their misery is upon them and they cannot
help themselves. They appeal to the King of
Morocco, but he is engaged in a great war with
the King of the Atlas and can give them neither
aid nor counsel.

My Cid hears of their plight and likes it well.
So he sets forth from Murviedro, marching by
night, and dawn finds him in the land of Monreal.
Thence he sends criers to Aragón and Navarre,
and envoys to Castile, bearing this message:

"Those who would no longer be poor but rich,
let them come and join My Cid, who plans to
take the field and lay siege to Valencia and win
her for Christendom. Let them come freely and
unforced. I shall tarry three days at Celfa del
Canal."

Thus said My Cid, the loyal Campeador, and
turned back to Murviedro, which was now his.

His message, know you, sped throughout the
land, and many men from noble Christendom,
thirsting after spoils, hastened to join him. The
word was everywhere noised about, and many
joined him and deserted him not.

My Cid, he of Bivar, grew in wealth, and when
he saw all his men gathering he was pleased.

My Cid Don Rodrigo tarries no longer, but
sets out for Valencia and falls upon it, investing
it so closely that none can escape, for he stops
all who would leave or enter. He gives those of

Valencia nine months in which to yield or find help. Nine full months, know you, he lies there, and at the tenth they yield.

Ah, how great was the rejoicing when My Cid won Valencia and entered the city! Those who had been on foot may now ride, and the gold and silver, who can count it? All his men are rich!

My Cid Don Rodrigo commands that his fifth be set apart. Thirty thousand marks fall to his lot, and other booty beyond the telling! Happy is My Cid, and happy are his men, when his standard is raised above the citadel!

While My Cid and his companies were resting, the King of Seville heard that Valencia had fallen defenseless, and he came to her aid with thirty thousand men. A battle was fought beyond the Garden of Valencia and My Cid, he of the great beard, put them to flight and pursued them well into Játiva. Ah, you should have seen the Moors as they fought against the current of the Júcar! And how they drank the water, although they thirsted not! The King of Seville escaped, thrice wounded.

My Cid returned with all his booty. What he took when he won the city was great, but this victory, know you, was more gainful still, for even the lowest ranks received a hundred marks of silver! You can see how the fame of our knight spread everywhere.

Great was the rejoicing among the Christians who were with My Cid Ruy Díaz, he who in a happy hour was born. His beard increased the

*epithet

while and grew longer, for My Cid had sworn an oath, saying:

"For the love of King Alfonso who banished me no scissors shall touch my beard, nor shall a single hair of it be cut, let Moors and Christians say what they will!"

My Cid Don Rodrigo rests at Valencia, with him Minaya Alvar Fáñez, who is ever at his side. Those who have shared his exile are now rich, for the illustrious Campeador has given them houses and lands in Valencia. Happy are they, for they see how great is the love that My Cid has for them, And those who joined him later, they are happy also.

But My Cid fears, as Minaya counsels him, that his men would take their spoils and return to Castile, if they could. So My Cid disposes that if any of his men leave without his permission they shall be seized, their goods forfeited, and they be hanged upon a gallows tree.

Thus he disposes, with the counsel of Minaya.

"And now, Minaya," said he, "if you think best, I will take a muster of those who are with me and have gained somewhat in my service. Let them all be counted, and if any one should hide himself or be reported missing, he shall forfeit his spoils to those of my vassals who stand guard in Valencia."

"Wisely spoken!" said Minaya.

My Cid then commanded all to gather in the city, and when they had done so he took a muster. Three thousand and six hundred men he counted, and he smiled and rejoiced in his heart.

"Thanks be to God, Minaya," he said, "and to our Holy Mother Mary! We had not so many when we left our town of Bivar! We are rich and we shall be richer! If it please you, Minaya, I will send you to Castile where our lands are. To King Alfonso, my natural lord, I wish to give a hundred horses from my share of the spoils. Offer him them and kiss his hands for me, and beg him, if he will, to let me have my wife Doña Ximena and my dear daughters. I will send for them, and do you say to him: 'Let the wife of My Cid and his young daughters be brought to these lands which we have won in foreign parts.'"

"Gladly!" said Minaya.

When they had thus spoken they made ready for Minaya's journey. My Cid gave him a hundred knights for his willing escort and sent a thousand silver marks to San Pedro de Cardeña, five hundred of them for Abbot Don Sancho.

At this time, to the great joy of all, it was learned that a tonsured priest was coming from the east whose name was Bishop Jerome, a man of letters and wise in all things, a good fighting man as well, on foot or horseback. He longed to face the Moors on the field of battle and urged My Cid to undertake further adventures against them, for, said he, if he did not take his fill of fighting, all Christendom would lament.

My Cid heard him and was pleased.

"Hear me now, Minaya Alvar Fáñez," he said. "By Our Father who is in heaven, and with His

favor, I will erect a bishopric in this land of
Valencia and give it to this good Christian! You
will bear these good tidings to Castile."

Alvar Fáñez rejoiced at the words of Don
Rodrigo, and forthwith they made Jerome bishop
in Valencia, where he would be rich.

God, how happy were the Christians to have a
lord bishop in Valencia! Happy also was Minaya
as he took his leave and departed.

The land of Valencia was now at peace, and
Minaya Alvar Fáñez set out for Castile. I will
not speak of the many stops he made. I do not
wish to count them. He inquired where he might
find King Alfonso, but the King had left for
Sahagún a little while before. So Minaya rode on
to Carrión, where the King was. Thither went
Minaya Alvar Fáñez, happy with his presents.

King Alfonso was coming from Mass when
Minaya Alvar Fáñez appeared and knelt with
noble mien in the presence of all the people. He
cast himself at King Alfonso's feet, kissed his
hands and said, well and prudently:

"A boon, my lord Alfonso, for the love of
God! My Cid the Campeador kisses your feet
and hands as his good lord and begs a boon, and
may God reward you! You cast him out of your
lands and withheld your love from him. He now
dwells in foreign parts, but he has not done badly.
He has won Jérica, and Onda the renowned; he
has taken Almenara and even the great Murviedro,
and likewise Puig and Castejón, and Benicadell,
a strong place. Besides all this, he has made him-

self king in Valencia and named a bishop there by his own authority. Five pitched battles has he fought, and won them all. Behold here the proof that I speak truly: a hundred war horses, swift and strong, all saddled and bridled. He kisses your hands and begs that you accept them, for he is your vassal and holds you for his lord."

The king raised his right hand and crossed himself.

"By St. Isidore!" he cried. "Glad am I in my heart that the Campeador has won such spoils! And happy am I at the great deeds the Campeador has done! I will receive these horses which he sends me for a gift."

The King was pleased, but not so Count García Ordóñez.

"It seems to me," said he, "that hardly a man can be left alive in the land of the Moors, the Campeador does so what he wills with them!"

"Hold your tongue, count!" said the King. "In every way he serves me better than you!"

Then up spoke Minaya, the noble one, and said:

"If it please you, O King, My Cid begs that he may take his wife, Doña Ximena, and his two daughters from the monastery where he left them, and bring them to Valencia."

"He has my glad consent," said the King. "I shall have them provided for while they are in my lands, and guarded from harm and dishonor. Once they are beyond the frontier, do you and the Campeador protect them. Hear me now, my companions and all my court. It is my will that the Campeador lose nothing, and I hereby restore to all who call him lord whatever I took from them. Let them enjoy their estates, wherever the Campeador may be. And I further undertake to protect them from harm and injury. This I do that they may serve their lord."

Minaya Alvar Fáñez kissed his hands, and the King smiled and nobly said:

"Those who would serve the Campeador have my leave to do so, and may God prosper them! We will gain more by this than by further punishment."

The Princes of Carrión then communed apart, saying:

"Great grows the fame of My Cid the Campeador! It might be well for us to marry his daughters, for our profit. Still, it would not be seemly for us to speak of this to him, because My Cid is merely lord of Bivar and we are the Princes of Carrión!"

But they said nothing of this to anyone and the matter rested there.

Minaya Alvar Fáñez then took his leave of the good King, who said:

"So soon, Minaya? May God's good grace go with you! My messenger will go with you also—he may be of service to you. If you take the ladies guard them well and give them whatever they may lack, as far as Medina, and let the Campeador protect them thereafter."

Minaya departed and the Princes of Carrión rode a little way with him.

"You are excellent in every way," they said, "be so now. Salute My Cid on our behalf and tell him he has our full support. My Cid will lose nothing if he loves us."

"That I can do without regret," replied Minaya.

The princes turned back and Minaya rode on to San Pedro where the ladies were. Ah, how pleased they were to see him! Minaya dismounted and stopped to pray at St. Peter's Church. His prayer done, he went to them and said:

"I salute you, Doña Ximena, and may God defend you and your two daughters! My Cid sends his greetings. I left him well and very rich. The King has granted me the honor of escorting you to Valencia, which now belongs to us. Ah, when My Cid sees you safe and well he will be so happy that he will never again feel pain!"

"God grant it!" said Doña Ximena.

Minaya Alvar Fáñez then dispatched three knights to My Cid at Valencia and said to them:

"Tell the Campeador (and may God keep him!) that the King has given his wife and daughters into my charge, and that while we are in Castile the King will provide for us, and that within the fortnight, God willing, I and his wife and daughters and all their ladies-in-waiting will be with him."

The knights departed on their errand and Minaya Alvar Fáñez remained at San Pedro de Cardeña. Ah, you should have seen the men gathering there, coming from all parts! They wish to join My Cid, he of Bivar, and beg Alvar Fáñez to help them.

"Gladly!" said Minaya.

Seventy-five knights thus were added to the hundred he had brought with him. A good escort for the ladies!

Minaya gave five hundred marks to Abbot Don Sancho. I will tell you now how he spent the other five hundred. The good Minaya thought to provide Doña Ximena and her daughters and the ladies who served them, with the best garments to be had in Burgos, and the best palfreys and mules. He did so and was about to leave when, behold, Raquel and Vidas came and threw themselves at his feet!

"A boon, Minaya!" they cried. "A boon, excellent knight! We are undone, know you, unless the Cid help us! We will relinquish our profit if he will return our capital."

"God willing, I shall speak of it to My Cid," replied Minaya. "You will surely be paid for what you have done for him."

"God grant it!" said Raquel and Vidas. "Otherwise, we shall leave Burgos and seek him out."

Minaya Alvar Fáñez returned to San Pedro, where many men joined him. He mounted, and great was the Abbot's grief when he took his leave.

"God go with you, Minaya Alvar Fáñez!" cried he. "Kiss the hands of the Campeador for me, and let him not forget this monastery in all the days of his life, for in its support My Cid does honor to himself."

"Gladly will I do so," replied Minaya.

They bade farewell to one another and Minaya's men mounted, in their company the royal messenger.

In all the land of King Alfonso they are well provided for. Five days are they upon the road from San Pedro to Medina, the ladies in the charge of Alvar Fáñez.

And now I will tell you of the knights who bore his message. My Cid, he of Bivar, heard it and rejoiced in his heart, saying:

"He who sends a good messenger may expect good news! Muño Gustioz, do you and Pedro Bermúdez, and Martín Antolínez, that loyal son of Burgos, and Bishop Jerome, that noble priest, do you all spur thither at once with a hundred knights, lest harm come to them. Go by way of Albarracín to Molina, which is somewhat farther on. It belongs to Abengalbón, my good friend, who will give you an escort of a hundred knights more. You will ride then to the land of Medina as speedily as you can, and there you will find my wife and daughters with Alvar Fáñez, as I am told. Bring them back to me with all honor. I will stay at Valencia, which I won at such great cost, for it would be folly to leave it unprotected. Here shall I stay, for Valencia is now my heritage!"

Thus spoke My Cid, and they mounted and

[handwritten margin note: I thought they weren't friends w/ the Moors?]

rode without stopping beyond Albarracín, resting at Bronchales. The next day brought them to Molina, where the Moor Abengalbón rode forth to meet them very joyfully.

"Are you indeed the vassals of my dear friend?" he cried. "Know you then that I am well pleased."

Muño Gustioz replied at once:

"My Cid salutes you and begs you to lend him a hundred knights. His wife and daughters are at Medina, and he would have you escort them hither, and even as far as Valencia, and leave them not."

"I shall be pleased!" said Abengalbón.

That night he spread for them a great feast and in the morning he mounted. He had been asked to give a hundred knights, but he gave two hundred. He crossed the mountains, rugged and lofty, and descended by the Valley of Arbujuelo to the Plain of Taranz, marching in such wise that he feared no one.

Minaya Alvar Fáñez, on guard at Medina, saw armed men approaching and sent two knights to discover who they were. The two rode boldly forth and one returned to Alvar Fáñez.

"It is the men of the Campeador," he said, "coming to meet us! Behold Pedro Bermúdez at their head, and Muño Gustioz, both dear friends of yours, and Martín Antolínez, he of Burgos, and Bishop Jerome, that loyal priest, and Abengalbón the castellan, who is bringing his own men for love of My Cid, to honor him! They march as one body and will soon be here."

"To horse, then!" cried Minaya.

The hundred tarry not, but mount. What a fine sight they make, their good horses covered with silken housings, bells jingling! They hang their shields about their necks and grasp their lances, pennants flying, that all the world may know that Alvar Fáñez is escorting the ladies from Castile in proper style!

The men who have been out scouting return and join them, and so great is their joy that they fall to jousting on the banks of the Jalón. Those of the Cid ride up and prostrate themselves at the feet of Minaya. Abengalbón smiles and embraces him, kissing him upon the shoulder, as is the Moorish custom.

"Well met, Minaya Alvar Fáñez!" he cried. "It is a great honor for us that you bring the wife of My Cid the Campeador and his daughters, and we all honor you. The Cid is a lucky man! Even if we loved him not we could not do him injury. In peace or war we shall share our goods with him. I hold him a fool who sees not that I speak truly!"

Minaya Alvar Fáñez smiled happily and said:

"In very truth, Abengalbón, you are his faithful friend! If, God willing, I see My Cid in life, you shall lose nothing by what you have done for him. But let us rest now, for our supper awaits us."

"Your hospitality is very welcome," replied Abengalbón. "Before three days have passed I shall return it twofold."

They enter Medina and Minaya serves them.

All are pleased with their fare, paid for by the King's messenger. Honored is My Cid in Valencia by the great feast given for him in Medina. The King pays for it all and Minaya pays nothing.

Night passed and morning came, and they heard Mass and mounted. They left Medina, crossed the Jalón, and spurred on up the river beyond Arbujuelo, over the Plain of Taranz, and came to Molina in the domain of Abengalbón. Bishop Jerome, that true Christian, guarded the ladies night and day, leading his good war horse, and another bearing his armor, Alvar Fáñez at his side.

They enter Molina, that fine rich city, where Abengalbón serves them well. They lack for nothing, and he even pays for shoeing their horses. And Minaya and the ladies, God, how he honors them! The next morning they mount again and ride on to Valencia, he serving them faithfully the while, and there the Moor takes his leave and will not permit them to pay him.

Thus joyfully and with such glad tidings do they approach within three leagues of Valencia and send word to My Cid, he who in a happy hour girded on his sword. Never was My Cid so happy, for he has word of those he most dearly loves. Two hundred knights does he send at a gallop to receive Minaya and the noble ladies, while he remains to defend Valencia, for well he knows that Minaya will guard them faithfully.

Behold now how they receive Minaya and the ladies and the little girls and the rest. My Cid

commands those of his household to defend the
citadel and the high towers and all the gates, and
the exits and the entrances, and to bring out
Babieca, his horse, which he won not long since
in battle from the King of Seville. My Cid knows
not whether Babieca will prove swift and stand
fast. At the gate of Valencia, now his, he wishes
to display his skill before his wife and daughters.

The ladies are received with great honor.
Bishop Jerome rides to the chapel and dismounts,
with all his company, and those who have time
to do so, don their surplices and with silver
crosses in their hands sally forth to receive the
ladies and the good Minaya.

He who in a happy hour was born tarries not,
but dons his silken tunic. Long is his beard!
Babieca is saddled and covered with his housing,
and My Cid mounts, armed with arms of wood.
He mounts his horse Babieca and rides so swiftly
that all are astonished. From that moment Babieca
is famous in all the land of Spain.

The run finished, My Cid dismounts and ap-
proaches his wife and his two daughters. Doña
Ximena throws herself at his feet.

"I thank you, O Campeador!" she cried. "You
have delivered me from shameful things. Behold
me here, my lord, and both your daughters, to
serve God and you! Gentle are they and good."

My Cid embraces the mother and her daugh-
ters, weeping in his joy. All his men rejoice like-
wise and take up their arms and fall to tilting.
Hear now what he says who in a happy hour
girded on his sword:

"Doña Ximena, my well-loved and honest wife, and you, the daughters of my heart and soul, come with me into Valencia, that city, into this patrimony I have won for you."

Mother and daughters kiss his hands and enter Valencia with great pomp. My Cid brings them to the citadel, to the very highest place, and they gaze about them with their lovely eyes. They see Valencia, how it spreads before them, and beyond it the sea, and there the Garden of Valencia, vast and thickly planted, and all things to delight them, and they raise their hands and give thanks to God for this gift, so rich and great.

My Cid and his companions were now free of care. Winter passed and March came round again. And now I will tell you of the news that came from beyond the sea, of Yusuf, that king, who was in Morocco.

The King of Morocco was vexed with My Cid Don Rodrigo.

"He has made himself strong in my lands," he said, "and he thanks no one for it but Jesus Christ!"

The King of Morocco gathered up all his forces, fifty thousand men, all armed. He is going to Valencia to seek out My Cid Don Rodrigo!

The ships land and his men disembark. They march on Valencia which My Cid has conquered. The infidel pitch their tents and make their camp. Such is the news that comes to My Cid.

"I thank Thee, O Spiritual Father!" he cried.

"All that I possess is here before me. With great hardship I took Valencia and I hold it as my heritage. I shall yield it up only with death! I thank God and His holy Mother Mary that my daughters and my wife are with me! Behold now this good fortune that comes to me from beyond the seas! I shall attack them, for I can do no other. My daughters and my wife shall see me fight, and learn how we make our living in this foreign land! With their own eyes they shall see me earn my bread!"

He brings his wife and daughters up to the citadel, and they raise their eyes and see the tents all pitched.

"What is this, My Cid, and God save you?"

"Fear not, my honest wife! These are riches, marvelous and great, that come to us. The Moors wish to make you a present, to celebrate your arrival, and as a dowry for your daughters!"

"I thank our Spiritual Father and you, O Cid!"

"And now, my wife, do you sit here in the citadel and fear not when you see me fight, for with the help of God and His holy Mother Mary I shall win this day. Ah, how my heart swells with pride to have you here to see me!"

The tents are pitched; dawn shines forth; drums loudly beat. My Cid rejoices and says:

"What a fine day this!"

His wife is so frightened that her heart almost bursts. Her ladies and her two daughters tremble also, for never since the day they were born have they felt such fear. But the good Cid, the Campeador, grasps his beard and says:

"Be not afraid, for all will go well. Within the fortnight, God willing, we shall take those drums for you and you will see how they are made. Then we will give them to Bishop Jerome to hang in the church of St. Mary Mother of God."

Such is the vow My Cid the Campeador makes.

The ladies, now reassured, are happy.

The Moors of Morocco ride swiftly and enter the Garden boldly. The lookout sees them and sounds the alarm. Ready are the men of My Cid Ruy Díaz! They joyfully arm and dash from the city. Wherever they encounter the Moors they attack them straightway and drive them rudely from the Garden. Five hundred of them, no less, do they slay that day and pursue the others to their very tents! They have done well and now ride back.

But Alvar Salvadórez has been taken captive! The men who eat the bread of My Cid tell him thereof, although he himself has seen it. My Cid is satisfied with them.

"Hear me now, my knights," he said, "and stop not on this account. This has been a good day and tomorrow will be a better. In the morning before daybreak you will all don your armor. Bishop Jerome will give you absolution and say Mass. Then to horse! We will strike them in the name of God and St. James. Indeed, we have no choice, for either we must win or they will take our bread."

And all reply:

"Gladly and bravely will we fight!"

Then up spoke Minaya and quickly said:

"Since such is your desire, O Cid, give me a hundred and thirty fighting knights, and when you attack I will strike them from the rear, and God will give the victory to one or the other of us, or perhaps to both."

"Granted!" said My Cid.

Day ends and night falls and the Christians arm themselves in haste. At the second cockcrow before dawn Bishop Jerome says Mass. Which done, he gives them absolution, saying:

"He who dies here facing the enemy, his sins will I take upon me and God will take his soul. My Cid Don Rodrigo, who in a happy hour girded on your sword, I said Mass for you this morning. Grant me now the honor of striking the first blow."

"You have it," said My Cid.

All, now armed, charge forth from the Towers of Cuarto, My Cid urging on his vassals. The gates are guarded by men of great prudence. My Cid leaps upon Babieca his horse, well accoutered. The standard is raised and they dash forth from Valencia. With My Cid at their head four thousand less thirty strike the fifty thousand with a will, while Alvar Alvarez and Minaya attack them from the rear. God is with them and they put the Moors to flight.

My Cid plies his lance until it breaks and then takes his sword and slays Moors without number, blood dripping from his elbow down. Thrice he strikes King Yusuf, who spurs away on his swift horse and takes refuge in the strong castle of Cullera, My Cid and his vassals in hot pursuit. Thence he turns back, he who in a happy hour was born, rejoicing at his victory. And now he sees the worth of Babieca, from head to tail!

All the spoils are in his hands. Of the fifty thousand Moors that they had counted but a hundred and four escape. The men of My Cid sack the camp and take, in gold and silver, three thousand marks, while the rest of the booty is beyond measure.

Happy is My Cid, and happy are his men, that God has given them this victory.

When My Cid sees that the King of Morocco is vanquished, he leaves Alvar Fáñez in command of the field and returns to Valencia with a hundred knights. Head bare, sword in hand, he rides into Valencia.

The ladies receive him and My Cid bows to them, reining in his horse.

"I salute you, ladies," he said, "and offer you these great spoils. While you held Valencia I won the field. It was the will of God and all His saints to give us this booty to celebrate your arrival. Behold my sword, all blood, and my horse, all sweat! It is thus that the Moors are beaten upon the field of battle. Pray God to vouchsafe me a few more years of life, and your honor will be great and men will come to kiss your hands!"

Thus said My Cid, speaking from his horse, and then dismounted. His wife and daughters and their ladies-in-waiting, seeing the Campeador on foot, knelt before him and said:

"We are yours, and may you live a thousand years!"

They go with him into the palace and sit with him upon the rich benches.

"Doña Ximena, my wife," he said, "did you not beg me once to give in marriage to my vassals these ladies who have so well served you? That I will do, and to each will I give a dowry of two hundred marks. Let this be known in Castile, where they have served so loyally. Of our daughters' marriage we must speak at greater length."

The ladies arise and kiss the Cid's hands, and great is the joy throughout the palace. As the Cid has commanded, so will it be done.

Minaya Alvar Fáñez is in the field with all his men. He writes back to make an accounting of his spoils. What with tents and arms and precious garments, he has gathered up an immense booty. I will tell you now the best of it. The richly caparisoned horses cannot be counted, for they are running loose and no one can catch them. The Moors of the countryside have taken some, but in spite of that a thousand horses of the finest fall to the lot of the Campeador. If so many fall to My Cid, how happy must the others be! Ah, how many rich tents and carved tent poles have My Cid and his vassals won! Two poles encrusted with gold support the tent of the King of Morocco. My Cid, the illustrious Campeador, commands that the tent be left standing and that no Christian touch it.

"I wish to send this tent," he said, "just as it

was brought from Morocco, to Alfonso the Castilian, in witness of what the Cid has won!"

With all their spoils they return to Valencia.

Bishop Jerome, that excellent priest, now sated with fighting with his hands, cannot count the Moors he has slain. Great is his share of the spoils, for My Cid Don Rodrigo, he who in a happy hour was born, has commanded that a tithe of all his fifth be given him.

Happy are the Christian men of Valencia, so rich are they in horses, arms, and money. Happy is Doña Ximena, happy are her two daughters, and happy are the other ladies, who consider themselves already married!

Then up spoke the good Cid and said:

"Where are you, famous one? Come to me, Minaya. You have well earned your share. Of this fifth of mine, I say, take what you will, and I will take what is left. Tomorrow without fail you will depart with some of these horses I have won, saddled and bridled, each with a sword. Two hundred of them will you give to King Alfonso, as a loving present from my wife and two daughters whom he sent to me, for they are beholden to him. And let him speak no ill of him who commands in Valencia!"

He tells Pedro Bermúdez to go with Minaya, and the next day in the morning they quickly mount, two hundred men in their company, with greetings for the King, whose hand My Cid kisses, and with two hundred horses as a memento of this battle which My Cid has won, and also this message:

"I shall serve him so long as I shall live!"

They set out from Valencia with the rich spoils which must be guarded. Day and night they ride without rest. They cross the mountains which divide the one land from the other and inquire for King Alfonso. They pass the mountains, forests, and rivers, and come to Valladolid, where King Alfonso is. Pedro Bermúdez and Minaya beg him to have their company met which is bringing presents from My Cid, he of Valencia.

Ah, you should have seen how happy was the King! He commands all the nobles to mount at once, himself at their head, and meet the messengers of him who in a happy hour was born. The Princes of Carrión, know you, are there, and Count García also, the Cid's wicked enemy. Some are pleased and others not. They see his men, and it seems to them an army rather than mere messengers. Even the King crosses himself.

Minaya and Pedro Bermúdez ride forward and dismount and kneel before King Alfonso. They kiss the earth and his feet.

"A boon, O gracious King!" they cried. "We kiss the earth and your feet in the name of My Cid the Campeador, who holds you his lord and himself your vassal. My Cid is beholden to you for the honor you have done him. A few days since, O King, he won a battle and put to flight the King of Morocco, Yusuf by name, and fifty thousand of his men. Immense were the spoils he took and all his men are rich. He kisses your hands and sends you these two hundred horses."

"Gladly will I receive them," said King Alfonso. "I thank My Cid who gives me such a present, and may I soon see the hour when I can requite him!"

Many are pleased at his words and kiss his hands, but Count García is very angry and calls ten of his kinsmen aside.

"It is a marvelous thing," he said, "how the Cid's honor increases! But the honor that he wins is an affront to us. He conquers kings on the battlefield as easily as if they were already dead and carries off their horses! This will bring us naught but grief!"

Then up spoke King Alfonso. Hear now what he said:

"I thank the Creator and St. Isidore for these two hundred horses that My Cid sends me, and I expect even greater services of him during the rest of my reign. Minaya Alvar Fáñez and Pedro Bermúdez, I command that you be richly dressed and given such arms as you may choose, that you may appear well in the eyes of Ruy Díaz, My Cid. Take now three of these horses. It seems to me, and my heart tells me so, that some good will come of this."

They kissed his hands and retired to rest, and all their needs were met.

And now I will tell you of the Princes of Carrión, who communed in secret together.

"My Cid's affairs go well!" they said. "Let us beg of him his two daughters in marriage, and thus we shall gain in honor and riches."

Whereupon they went to King Alfonso and said:

"We beg a boon of you, O King and lord. If it please you, we beg that you ask for us the hands of the daughters of the Campeador. We would marry them, for their honor and our advantage."

The King thought for a long hour and said:

"I banished the good Campeador from my lands. I did him wrong and he repays me with great good. I know not whether he will like your proposal, but, since that is your desire, let us approach him with it."

He then called Minaya Alvar Fáñez and Pedro Bermúdez to him and withdrew with them to another room.

"Hear me now, Minaya," he said, "and you, Pedro Bermúdez. My Cid Ruy Díaz the Campeador serves me well. I shall pardon him, as he deserves. Let him come to see me, if he so wishes, for I have news for him at this court of mine. Diego and Fernando, the Princes of Carrión, beg the hands of his two daughters in marriage. Do you be my good messengers and say to the Campeador that he will gain in honor thereby, having as sons-in-law the Princes of Carrión."

Minaya answered, and Pedro Bermúdez approved his words:

"We shall repeat your message to the Cid and he will do as he thinks best."

"Moreover," said the King, "tell My Cid Ruy Díaz, he who in a happy hour was born, that I shall meet with him at whatever spot he chooses upon the frontier, for I wish to favor My Cid as far as in me lies."

They take their leave of the King and with

his message set out for Valencia with all their men.

My Cid heard that they were coming and quickly mounted and went to greet them. My Cid smiled and warmly did he embrace them.

"So you have returned, Minaya!" he cried. "And you, Pedro Bermúdez! Two such knights can be found in no other land! How does my lord Alfonso? Was he pleased with my gift?"

"In his very heart," answered Minaya, "and he has restored you to his love."

"Now God be thanked!" said My Cid.

They told him then of the proposal of Alfonso of León, that My Cid give his daughters in marriage to the Princes of Carrión, for thus would he gain in honor and wealth. Moreover, they said, the King strongly urged him to accept.

My Cid the good Campeador heard and long did he meditate.

"I give thanks to Our Lord Jesus!" he said. "I was banished from the land and all my honors were taken from me. With much hardship did I win what I now possess. I thank God that I have regained the love of my King and that he begs of me the hands of my daughters for the Princes of Carrión! But tell me now, Minaya, and you, Pedro Bermúdez, what think you of this marriage?"

"What pleases you will please us also," they replied.

"The Princes of Carrión," said the Cid, "are of great estate and have a very proud place at court. I like not this marriage, but he urges it who is greater than I. Let us speak of this only amongst ourselves. God is in His heaven and will tell us what is best to do."

"King Alfonso also says that he will come to meet you wherever you like, for he wishes to see you and prove his love. Then you can decide what you should do."

"I shall be happy to meet with him," said the Cid.

"Consider then," said Minaya, "where it shall be."

"If the King so commands," replied My Cid, "we shall seek him out wherever he may be. What he wishes, that shall be our desire also. Let us meet him, then, upon the Tagus, that great river, whenever it pleases my lord."

The letters are written and strongly sealed, and are sent forthwith by the hands of two knights. Whatever the King desires, that will the Campeador do.

The letters were delivered to the honest King, who rejoiced in his heart when he saw them and said:

"Salute My Cid for me, he who in a happy hour girded on his sword, and tell him that I shall see him within these three weeks, if I live. I shall not fail him."

The messengers tarried not, but returned to My Cid.

On both sides preparations are made for the meeting. Never in Castile were so many handsome mules seen, or so many swift palfreys and great war horses and speedy, so many pennants flying from good lances, so many shields with bosses of gold and silver, so many skins and mantles and good silken garments of Alexandria! The King commands that a great store of provisions be sent to the River Tagus, where the meeting is to be, and the King goes thither with many goodly companies. The Princes of Carrión are so happy that they make new debts here and pay old ones there, thinking to increase their wealth with all the gold and silver they desire.

King Alfonso rides in haste, and counts and potentates and great companies ride with him. The Princes of Carrión bring also many men. Companies from León and Galicia escort the King, and the Castilians, know you, are without number. All gallop toward the meeting place.

In Valencia My Cid tarries not, but sets forth, bringing with him many sleek mules and excellent palfreys, many good arms and swift war horses, many fine capes and mantles and skins. All, great and humble, are dressed in colors.

Minaya Alvar Fáñez, and Pedro Bermúdez, and Martín Muñoz, who commanded at Monte Mayor, and Martín Antolínez, the illustrious one of Burgos, and Bishop Jerome, that best of priests, and Alvar Alvarez, and Alvar Salvadórez, and Muño Gustioz, that fine knight, and Galindo García, he of Aragón, all these make ready to accompany the Campeador, as do all the others.

Alvar Salvadórez and Galindo García, he of Aragón, these two the Campeador appoints to stand faithful guard over Valencia and those he leaves behind. The gates of the castle My Cid commands shall not be opened day or night, for within are his wife and daughters, whom he loves with all his heart and soul, and the ladies who serve them well. He also commands, like the prudent man he is, that none of them leave the castle until he returns.

They spur forth from Valencia, leading the chargers, great and swift, that My Cid has won, and not cheaply! He is going to meet the King!

King Alfonso had arrived the day before. His men see the good Campeador approaching and go forth to meet him with every honor. When he who in a happy hour was born sees the King he commands that all save those knights he most dearly loves stay where they are, while he dismounts with his fifteen companions, as he has provided. Then does he cast himself upon the ground and pluck a mouthful of grass, weeping in his great joy. Thus he pays homage to King Alfonso, his lord, and falls at his feet.

King Alfonso was much grieved at this and said:

"Arise, My Cid the Campeador, and kiss my hands, but not my feet! If you obey me not, you will not regain my love!"

But My Cid remained upon his knees and cried:

"A boon, my natural lord! Give me your love as I am and let all those present hear you!"

"That will I do," replied the King, "with all my heart and soul! I hereby forgive you, and from this day forward you are welcome to all my kingdom!"

Then up spoke My Cid and said:

"I thank you, my lord Alfonso! First I thank God in His heaven and then you, and all these men who surround us."

Still kneeling, he kissed the King's hands, and then arose and kissed his mouth. All rejoiced to see it, save only Alvar Díaz and García Ordóñez, who were angry.

Then said My Cid:

"I thank God Our Father that I have regained the love of my lord Alfonso! God will never abandon me day or night! Be my guest today, my lord, if it please you."

"That would not be just," replied the King. "You have but now arrived, while we arrived last night. You shall be my guest today, O Cid Campeador, and tomorrow it shall be as you wish."

My Cid kissed the King's hands and assented.

And now the Princes of Carrión came and knelt before him.

"We salute you, O Cid," they said, "born in a happy hour, and we shall favor you in whatever way we can."

"God grant it!" replied My Cid.

My Cid was that day the guest of the King, who left not his side, so much did he love him. All were astonished, gazing upon his beard, so quickly had it grown.

The day passed and night fell. The next morning the sun shone brightly forth and the Campeador commanded his men to prepare a feast for all, and so well did he serve them that they agreed that not in three years past had they eaten so well.

The next morning, just at sunrise, Bishop Jerome sang Mass, and after Mass all gathered together to hear the King, who thus addressed them:

"Hear me now, my companies, my counts and knights. I wish to beg a favor of My Cid the Campeador, and may Jesus Christ give him joy in it! I beg you, O Cid, to give your daughters, Doña Elvira and Doña Sol, to the Princes of Carrión, to be their wedded wives, for it seems to me that such a union would be both honorable and advantageous. They beg them of you, and such is my desire. And let all those here, mine as well as yours, join me in my petition. Give us them, O Cid, and God be with you!"

"It is not meet," replied the Campeador, "that I should give my daughters in marriage, for they are young and few in days. The Princes of Carrión are of high estate and worthy of my daughters and even better. I begot my daughters; you reared them. They and I are yours to command. Doña Elvira and Doña Sol are in your hands, O King. Give them to whom you please and I shall be content."

"I thank you and all my court!" said the King.

Then arose the Princes of Carrión and kissed the hands of him who in a happy hour was born, and exchanged swords with him in the presence of King Alfonso.

Then up spoke King Alfonso, like the noble lord he was.

"I thank you, good Cid, favored of God, for

thus giving me the hands of your daughters for the Princes of Carrión, and I hereby give Doña Elvira and Doña Sol to them to be their wedded wives. With your consent, O Cid, do I bestow your daughters' hands upon them, and may it please God that you have joy of it! The Princes of Carrión are now your sons and will go with you. I return to Castile. I shall make them a wedding present of three hundred marks, or for whatever purpose you please. Once your daughters and sons-in-law are in your domain of great Valencia, they all will be your children and will obey you, Campeador."

My Cid kissed the King's hands.

"Much do I thank you, my King and lord!" he said. "But it is you who give my daughters in marriage, not I."

Promises were then exchanged and pledges made, for the next morning at sunrise each was to return whence he had come.

And now My Cid did a wonderful thing. All those sleek mules and excellent palfreys, and all those precious garments, he gave to those who wished them, denying none. Sixty horses he gave as gifts, and all who were at the meeting were well pleased with him. And now they would depart, for night had fallen.

The King then took the Princes of Carrión by the hand and gave them into the authority of My Cid the Campeador.

"Behold your sons," said he, "for they are now your sons-in-law. Henceforth, O Cid, you will treat them as your sons, and they will serve you as their father and respect you as their lord."

"I thank you, O King," replied My Cid, "and I accept your gift. May God in His heaven reward you! And now I beg a boon of you, my King and natural lord. You have given my daughters in marriage, according to your desire. I beg you now to name your delegate to whom I may release them, for I shall not give them by my own hand, lest it be boasted of."

"Here is Alvar Fáñez," said the King. "Minaya, do you take the Cid's daughters and give them to the counts, as I do now in their absence. You will stand for me at their wedding and when we meet again you will tell me how you did."

"Willingly, my lord," said Alvar Fáñez.

All this was carried out, know you, with great diligence.

"And now, King Alfonso, my honored lord," said My Cid, "be pleased to accept a remembrance of this meeting of ours. I have brought you thirty palfreys, well saddled and bridled, and thirty swift war horses as well, likewise equipped. Receive this gift, my lord, and I kiss your hands."

Then said King Alfonso:

"You do too much! I accept your gift, and may it please God and all His saints to reward you for it! You have greatly honored me, My Cid Ruy Díaz. You serve me well and I am pleased. If I live I shall requite you. To God I now commend you, for I am departing hence, and may He bring this to a happy end!"

My Cid vaulted upon Babieca his horse and said:

"Here in the presence of my lord King Alfonso, I say that all who would attend the wedding and have gifts of me, let them come with me and they will profit therefrom."

My Cid then bade farewell to his lord King Alfonso and, not wishing the King to ride with him, he quickly rode away.

Ah, you should have seen all those brave knights come up to kiss the King's hands and beg their leave of him!

"A boon!" they cried. "Permit us to go to great Valencia, to the domain of My Cid, and be present at the wedding of the Princes of Carrión with the daughters of My Cid, Doña Elvira and Doña Sol."

The King was pleased to consent, and so the company of the Cid increased, while that of the King diminished, so many went with the Campeador.

All set forth for Valencia, which My Cid had won in a happy hour, and he named Pedro Bermúdez and Muño Gustioz as escorts for Fernando and Diego—none better in all the Cid's household!—for they knew the ways of the Princes of Carrión. With them went Asur González, quarrelsome and loose of tongue, and otherwise of little worth. All did honor to the Princes of Carrión.

Behold them now in the land of Valencia, won by My Cid, and their joy increases as they near the city. Then said My Cid to Don Pedro and Muño Gustioz:

"Find you now a lodging for the Princes of Carrión and stay with them, I command you, and tomorrow at sunrise they shall see their wives, Doña Elvira and Doña Sol."

The princes went to their lodging that night and My Cid the Campeador entered into the palace, where he was received by Doña Ximena and his two daughters.

"And have you indeed returned!" cried she. "O Campeador who in a happy hour girded on your sword! May you be with us for many days!"

"I thank God that I am here, my honest wife!" he said. "I have brought you two sons-in-law who will do us honor. You may thank me, my daughters, for I have found good husbands for you."

His wife and daughters kissed his hands, as did the ladies who served them.

"We thank our Creator and you, O Cid of the noble beard!" said Doña Ximena. "All that you do is well done! While you live, our daughters will never want!"

"How rich we shall be when we are married!" cried Doña Elvira and Doña Sol.

"Doña Ximena, my wife," said My Cid, "I thank God for it! And to you, my daughters, I say that with this marriage of yours our honor will be increased. But bear in mind that it was not I who arranged it; but my lord Don Alfonso begged you of me so strongly and with such good will that I could not refuse him and gave you both into his hands. Believe me, then, he it was who gave your hands in marriage, not I."

Now they make the palace ready. Floors and walls are covered with many purple and silken tapestries and precious hangings. Ah, you would have been happy to be in the palace and eat there!

All the knights are summoned, and the Princes of Carrión as well. They come riding to the palace, dressed in rich array and adorned all in their best. They dismount and enter with great decorum. God, how humbly do they enter! My Cid and all his vassals receive them, and they bow to him and his wife and seat themselves upon the precious benches. Those of My Cid are no less polite, while they watch him who in a happy hour was born.

The Campeador then rose to his feet and said:

"We have this to do, so why tarry? Come to me, Alvar Fáñez, you whom I love and cherish. Behold here both my daughters; I give them into your hands. As well you know, this I asked of the King, and I shall not fail him in anything we there agreed upon. With your own hands give my daughters to the Princes of Carrión. They have my blessing and let us have done with it."

"Gladly will I do so," said Minaya.

Then arose Doña Elvira and Doña Sol, and Minaya gave them into the hands of the Princes of Carrión.

"Brothers both," he said, "Minaya stands before you. By order of the King, who thus commanded me, I give to you these noble ladies whom you will take as your lawful wedded wives."

The counts received them joyfully and kissed the hands of My Cid and his wife.

Which done, all left the palace and rode swiftly to St. Mary's Church, where Bishop Jerome donned his priestly robes in haste and stood waiting for them at the door. He gave them then his blessing and sang Mass. Whereupon all left the church and quickly spurred to the tilting field of Valencia. God, how well tilted My Cid and his vassals! Three times he changed horses, he who in a happy hour was born.

My Cid was pleased with what he saw there, for the Princes of Carrión rode well.

These with their wives then rode back to Valencia.

Rich was the wedding in the great palace!

The next morning My Cid had seven targets erected in the tilting field and before breakfast they were all demolished.

A full fortnight lasted the wedding feast, and toward its end the nobles began to depart. My Cid gave them as gifts no fewer than a hundred palfreys and mules and swift war horses, and skins and mantles and many garments, and the money he gave them was beyond the telling. My Cid's vassals also did their part and gave to each his gift. He who desired wealth received aplenty and all who had come to the wedding returned rich to Castile.

The guests departed and took their leave of Ruy Díaz, he who in a happy hour was born, and of all the ladies and nobles as well. Happy did they depart from My Cid and his vassals, speaking well of them, as was just. And happy were Diego and Fernando, those sons of Count Gonzalo.

The wedding guests depart for Castile and My Cid remains in Valencia with his sons-in-law, who abide there for two full years, in the midst of loving care.

Happy are My Cid and all his vassals! May St. Mary and God Our Holy Father grant that My Cid and he who arranged this marriage have reason to rejoice thereat!

And now I have come to the end of my canto, and may the Creator and all His saints watch over you!

III

THE OUTRAGE
AT CORPES

MY CID REMAINED IN VALENCIA
with all his men, with him also his sons-
in-law, the Princes of Carrión.

Now, the Campeador was sleeping upon a
bench when, know you, a fearsome thing hap-
pened. A lion escaped from his cage and broke
his bonds, causing consternation in the court. My
Cid's men forthwith seized their mantles and sur-
rounded the bench upon which their lord was
lying, but Fernando González, one of the Princes
of Carrión, vainly sought a place of safety. Not
an open chamber or tower could he find, but
hid beneath the Cid's bench, so fearful was he!
And Diego González, his brother, ran out the
door, shouting:

"I shall never see Carrión again!"

Whereupon he took refuge behind the wine
press, and such was his terror that he quite de-
filed his tunic and mantle.

Then he who in a happy hour was born awoke
and saw his bench surrounded by his good
knights.

"What is this, my companions?" he asked.
"And what are you doing here?"

"Your lion, honored lord!" they answered.
"Your lion has escaped!"

Then did My Cid arise, his mantle still about
him, and approach the lion, and the lion cowered

before him, resting his muzzle upon the floor. And My Cid seized him by the mane and thrust him back into his cage, as if leading him by a halter, to the great wonderment of those who saw it.

My Cid then inquired for his sons-in-law, but they could not be found and answered not when they were called. And when they were found, so pale were they that never in the court was such laughter heard as then burst out, until My Cid forbade it. The Princes of Carrión held themselves affronted thereby, so bitterly did they resent what had happened.

While they were thus sulking, behold, an army came from out of Morocco and laid siege to Valencia. Fifty thousand Moors of the noblest were they, commanded by King Búcar, of whom you have heard tell. They halted in the field of Cuarto and there pitched their tents.

The Cid and all his knights rejoiced, for this would increase their wealth, God willing. But, know you, the Princes of Carrión were stricken in their hearts, seeing all those Moorish tents and liking them not at all. The two brothers withdrew and thus communed together:

"Ah, we have given too much thought to our gain in this business and not enough to our loss! Now must we do battle and shall never again see Carrión! The daughters of the Cid will be widows!"

Muño Gustioz overheard them speaking thus in secret and brought word of it to the Campeador, saying:

"Behold now these sons-in-law of yours, how bold they are! And how they wish themselves back in Carrión and out of this battle! Do you go comfort them, and God help you! Tell them to stay at home and take no part in the fighting, for with you at our head, and with the help of God, we shall win this day!"

My Cid Don Rodrigo smiled and approached the princes.

"God save you, my sons-in-law, O Princes of Carrión!" he said. "In your arms you hold my daughters two, white as the sun. I wish to go forth and do battle; you, to return to Carrión. Do you then remain in Valencia and take your pleasure, for I know how to deal with these Moors and shall drive them out, with God's help."

[Now, while they were thus speaking, King Búcar sent word to the Cid to abandon Valencia and go in peace. Otherwise, he said, the Cid would pay dearly for all that he had done. But the Cid answered the messenger, saying:

"Do you return and tell Búcar, that son of our enemies, that within three days I will pay him what he asks."

The next day the Cid commanded his men to arm, and marched against the Moors. The Princes of Carrión begged that he allow them to be among the first to attack. The Cid formed his lines and Fernando, one of the princes, rode forth to do battle with a Moor named Aladraf. The Moor saw him approaching and spurred to meet him, but the prince, in great fear, turned tail and fled.

Pedro Bermúdez, who was with the prince, attacked the Moor and slew him. Then, taking the Moor's horse, he spurred after the flying prince and said:

"Don Fernando, do you take this horse and tell the others that you slew its master, and I will bear you witness."

"Much do I thank you, Don Pedro Bermúdez," replied the prince], "and may I soon see the hour when I can repay you twofold!"

The two returned together and Don Pedro testified to the deed of which Fernando boasted, and My Cid and all his vassals were pleased with him.

"These sons-in-law of mine," said My Cid, "if it please God Our Father, will yet prove themselves in battle!"

He spoke, his men advanced, and the Moorish drums beat loudly. Many of the Christians, newly arrived, were astonished, for they had never heard the like, but even more dismayed were Diego and Fernando, who unwillingly were there.

Hear now what he said who in a happy hour was born:

"Ho there, Pedro Bermúdez, my dear nephew, do you watch after Diego and Fernando, my sons-in-law whom I cherish. The Moors, God helping us, shall not win the day!"

"If you love me, O Cid," replied Pedro Bermúdez, "I say let me not be the princes' guardian this day. Let him who will look after them, for they are nothing to me. I and my men wish to attack in the van. Do you and yours remain in the rear. If things go badly with me, you may come to my aid."

Then up spoke Alvar Fáñez and said:

"Hear me, My Cid, O loyal Campeador. God will give us victory, with your help, O worthy one, favored of Him! Command us to strike where you think best, and each of us will do his duty. With God's help and your good luck, we shall see what we shall see!"

"Calmly, calmly!" said My Cid.

Behold now Bishop Jerome, how well armed is he! He stands before the lucky one and says:

"I sang for you today the Mass of the Holy Trinity. I left my country and sought you out, thinking to slay a few Moors. I wish to bring honor to my order and my hands by being the first to strike. My pennant bears my coat of arms and, please God, I wish to prove them, that my heart may rejoice and you be pleased with me. If you grant me not this boon I shall leave you!"

"Be it as you wish," replied My Cid. "Behold, the Moors are here before you. Now let us see how our bishop fights!"

Bishop Jerome spurs to the attack and fights his way to the very edge of the Moorish encampment. With the help of God who loves him, and his good luck, he slays two Moors at the first onset and breaks his lance. Whereupon he grasps his sword and deals mighty blows with it. God, how well does the bishop fight! Two he slays with his lance and five with his sword. But the

Moors are many and surround him. They strike him heavy blows, but cannot pierce his armor.

He who in a happy hour was born, seeing the bishop's plight, embraces his shield and lowers his lance, spurring Babieca, his swift horse, and striking the enemy with a will. The Campeador breaks through the front ranks, unhorsing seven, four of whom he slays. It pleases God to give him the victory. The Moors retreat and My Cid and his men pursue them. Ah, you should have seen the men of My Cid breaking all those tent ropes, pulling up the stakes, and felling the carved poles! The men of My Cid drive those of Búcar from their encampment.

They drive them from their tents and pursue them. Ah, you should have seen the many arms lopped off, still sheathed in mail, the many heads, still wearing their helmets, rolling in the dust, the many horses running riderless! Seven full miles do they pursue them, and My Cid overtakes King Búcar.

"Turn back, O Búcar," he cried, "you who came from beyond the sea! It is I, the Cid, he of the great beard, with whom you must deal now! Let us kiss and be friends!"

But Búcar replied:

"God's curse upon such friendship! You have your sword in hand and I see you spurring after me. It could be that you think to flesh it in my body! But if my horse stumble not, nor fall with me, you will overtake me only in the sea!"

"Not so!" said My Cid.

Good is Búcar's horse and swiftly does he run,

but My Cid's Babieca slowly gains on him. At three fathoms from the water My Cid overtakes King Búcar and, raising his sword Colada, deals him a mighty blow which shears the rubies from his helmet, cuts through the helmet itself, and opens the Moor's body to the waist.

My Cid has slain Búcar, that king from beyond the sea, and won his sword Tizón, worth a thousand marks of gold! Thus does My Cid win this marvelous great battle, with honor for himself and all his men. They sack the camp thoroughly, know you, and come to the tent of him who in a happy hour was born.

My Cid Ruy Díaz, the renowned Campeador, bearing the two swords which he cherishes, gallops back from the slaughter, his face uncovered, helmet and hood removed. His vassals ride in from all directions. And now My Cid sees a thing which pleases him, for he raises his eyes and beholds Diego and Fernando approaching, those sons of Count Gonzalo, and he smiles happily and says:

"Is it you, my sons-in-law? Now you are my sons indeed! I know that you are well pleased to fight, and this good word will be brought to Carrión, how we have vanquished King Búcar. As I trust in God and all His saints, we shall not lose by this great victory!"

Then up came Minaya Alvar Fáñez, his shield about his neck, all dented, although of lance thrusts bore he no mark, for none had touched him. Blood dripped from his elbow down, for he had slain above a score of Moors.

"Thank God Our Father who is in heaven!" cried he. "And thank you, O Cid, who in a happy hour were born! You have slain Búcar and the field is ours, with all these spoils for you and your vassals! Your sons-in-law have likewise proved their worth, taking their fill of fighting Moors upon the field of battle."

"I am well pleased with them," said My Cid. "They were good today and tomorrow they will be excellent."

My Cid spoke in praise of them, but they thought he mocked them.

All the spoils are brought to Valencia, and My Cid is happy, as are all his vassals, for to the lot of each will fall six hundred marks of silver!

Now, the sons-in-law of My Cid, when they receive their share of the spoils and have it in their hands, think they will never again be poor so long as they shall live, and those of Valencia bedeck themselves with rich skins and good mantles. Happy are My Cid and his vassals! What a great day in the court of the Campeador when he wins the battle and slays King Búcar! My Cid raised his hand and stroked his beard.

"I give thanks to Jesus Christ, Lord of this world," he said, "that I have seen at last what I so desired, my two sons-in-law fighting at my side! Their fame will reach Carrión, how they have brought honor to themselves and me!"

Immense is the booty that My Cid's men now have, with what they took before and what they have won this day. My Cid, he who in a happy hour was born, commands that all receive their just share of the spoils of battle, and that his own fifth be not overlooked, and his men prudently obey him. To the lot of My Cid fall six hundred horses, and the pack animals and camels cannot be counted. Such are the spoils taken by My Cid!

"I thank the Lord God!" cried he. "I once was poor, but now am rich! I have goods and lands and gold, and honor too, for the Princes of Carrión are my sons-in-law! I have won battles when it pleased God to aid me, and Moors and Christians live in fear of me. Even in Morocco, where the mosques are, they dread lest some night I fall upon them, although I intend it not. I shall not seek them out, but remain in Valencia, and they, God willing, shall pay me tribute."

Great is the rejoicing in Valencia among the companions of the Campeador because of this battle which they have so bravely fought. And great is the joy of his two sons-in-law, for their share of the spoils comes to five thousand marks! The Princes of Carrión are now rich men indeed!

They and the others come to the court where My Cid is, with Bishop Jerome and good Alvar Fáñez, that fighting knight, and many more of My Cid's household. The Princes of Carrión enter and Minaya receives them in the name of My Cid the Campeador.

"Welcome, my brothers!" cried he. "You honor us!"

Pleased is My Cid that they have come.

"My sons," he said, "behold here my noble wife and my two daughters, Doña Elvira and

Doña Sol. Let them embrace you and serve you with all their hearts. I thank God and St. Mary, Mother of Our Lord, for this union by which you have gained in honor! Good tidings of this day will come to the lands of Carrión!"

And Prince Fernando replied:

"I thank our Creator and you, noble Cid, for these great riches that we cannot count! We have won much honor in your service. We have vanquished Moors on the field of battle and slain King Búcar, that proven traitor. Think now of your own portion, for what is ours is in safe hands."

The vassals of My Cid smiled at this, for some had fought more valiantly and others had joined in the pursuit, but none had seen Diego and Fernando in that battle.

Resentful of the jests of which they are now the butt, and of the ridicule heaped upon them day and night, the princes now conceive a wicked plan. They withdraw, these two worthy brothers, and all unwillingly do we listen to what they say.

"Let us depart for Carrión," said one, "for we have stayed too long. Such is the wealth that we have won that we cannot spend it in all the days of our lives. Let us beg the Campeador to give us our wives, that we may bring them to the lands of Carrión and show them their heritage. We shall take them away from Valencia, away from the protection of the Campeador, and upon the journey we shall have our pleasure of them, before they mock us with that matter of the lion.

We are the Princes of Carrión! We are now rich and can teach a lesson to these daughters of the Campeador!"

"With our wealth," said the other, "we are now great nobles and a fitting match for the daughters of kings or emperors! Are we not indeed the rightful Princes of Carrión? We shall shame the daughters of the Campeador before they mock us with the lion!"

Having thus formed their plan, they returned, and Fernando González spoke, imposing silence upon the court:

"God keep you, O Cid Campeador! And may it please Doña Ximena and you, and Alvar Fáñez and all those here present, to let us take our wives, with your blessing, and bring them to our lands of Carrión, where we shall put them in possession of the wedding portion which we gave them. Thus will your daughters see our lands and the patrimony of our children."

My Cid the Campeador, all unsuspecting, replied:

"I shall give you not only my daughters, but something of my own besides. You gave them cities in your lands of Carrión for their wedding portion. I shall give them for their household three thousand marks, and mules and palfreys, sleek and fine, and war horses, swift and strong, and many garments of wool and silk, shot with golden threads. And to you I shall give my two swords, Colada and Tizón, won, as well you know, in equal battle. You have my daughters now, and I hold you as my sons. Ah, you are taking from me the very stuff of my heart! Let those of Galicia, Castile, and León know what great wealth you bring to them! Cherish these daughters of mine, O princes, for they are now your wives. If you serve them well I shall reward you fittingly."

The Princes of Carrión give their promise and take the daughters of the Campeador, and receive the presents that he has commanded be given them. The princes have now all the wealth they can desire and order that it be loaded upon their mules.

Great is the excitement in noble Valencia, and all take up their arms and ride forth from the city. The daughters of the Cid are going to Carrión!

Doña Elvira and Doña Sol are ready to mount and depart, but first they come and kneel before the Cid Campeador.

"Father," they said, "we beg a boon of you, and may God preserve you! You begot us and our mother bore us. We kneel before you both, our mistress and lord. You are sending us forth to the lands of Carrión, and it is our duty to do what you command; but we beg that you forget us not there in the lands of Carrión."

My Cid embraced them both and kissed them upon the mouth. Their mother embraced and kissed them also, and said:

"Go now, my daughters, and may God keep you! You have my blessing and your father's. You are going to Carrión, your heritage, and now I know I have married you well."

Doña Elvira and Doña Sol kissed the hands of their father and mother, who blessed them.

And now My Cid and his men ride forth, bravely arrayed, displaying their arms and horsemanship. The Princes of Carrión depart from Valencia the illustrious, bidding farewell to the ladies-in-waiting and their companions. All ride through the Garden of Valencia, tilting as they go. Joyful are My Cid and his men.

But he who in a happy hour was born feels in his heart that all may not be well with this union. Too late does he repent, for his daughters are wedded now.

"Where are you, Félix Muñoz, my nephew?" said he. "You are my daughters' dear cousin. Go, I command you, to Carrión and see this heritage of theirs. Then you will return and tell me what you have learned."

"Right gladly will I do so," said Félix Muñoz.

Then up came Alvar Fáñez and stood before My Cid.

"Let us return to great Valencia, O Cid," said he, "for if it please God Our Father we shall see your daughters one day in the lands of Carrión."

Then said My Cid:

"Doña Elvira and Doña Sol, to God I now commend you. Do you so conduct yourselves that I have pleasure in you."

"God grant it!" said his sons-in-law.

Great is the lamentation at their parting. Father and daughters weep with grief, and the knights of the Campeador weep also.

"Hear me now, Félix Muñoz, my nephew," said My Cid. "You will pass through Molina and stop there for one night. Salute my friend, the Moor Abengalbón, and beg him to receive my sons-in-law with all honor. Tell him I am sending my daughters to the lands of Carrión and beg him to serve them in whatever they may need and escort them as far as Medina for love of me. I shall reward him well for all he does."

They parted as the nail is parted from the flesh.

He who in a happy hour was born turned back to Valencia and the Princes of Carrión went their way. Their first day's journey brought them to Albarracín, whence they spurred on and came to Molina, where Abengalbón was. The Moor learned of their coming and rejoiced and rode forth to meet them in great excitement. God, how well he served them with all his heart! The next day in the morning he rode with them, in his company an escort of two hundred knights. They crossed the mountains called the Sierra de Luzón and descended by the valley of Arbujuelo, resting that night on the Jalón at a place called Ansarera.

The Moor gave presents to the daughters of the Cid, and a good horse each to the Princes of Carrión—all this for the love he bore the Cid Campeador.

The two brothers saw the riches that the Moor brought forth and plotted a wicked thing.

"We are going to abandon the daughters of the Cid," they said. "Why not, then, kill the Moor

Abengalbón as well, and all his riches will be ours? They will be ours as surely as we hold our lands of Carrión, and the Cid Campeador cannot call us to account!"

While those of Carrión were thus treacherously plotting, lo, a Moor who knew their language overheard them. He kept not silent but told it all to Abengalbón.

"My lord castellan," he said, "beware the Princes of Carrión! They plot your death!"

The Moor Abengalbón, a brave man, mounted forthwith, the two hundred knights of his company doing mock battle the while, and rode up to the Princes of Carrión, and what the Moor said to them pleased them not. Said he:

"Were it not for the love I bear My Cid the Campeador I would pay you off in such wise that it would resound throughout the land! Then I would bring back his daughters to the loyal Campeador and you would never again see your lands of Carrión! Tell me now, O Princes of Carrión, what have I done that you should plot my death? Have I not served you faithfully? Get you gone, treacherous rascals that you are! Doña Elvira and Doña Sol, by your leave I will now depart, for I hold in small esteem the renown of those of Carrión. And may God, Lord of all the world, grant that My Cid have joy of this union!"

So saying, the Moor turned away. He crossed the Jalón and went back to Molina, like the prudent man he was, doing mock battle the while with his men.

The Princes of Carrión departed from Ansarera and rode day and night. To their left they passed Atienza, a strong high place, and the Sierra de Miedes, and spurred on through Montes Claros. To their left they passed Griza, founded by Alamos, and the caves where he had held Elfa a prisoner. To their right, farther on, was San Esteban, whence they entered into the oaken woods of Corpes, with its trees so tall they brush the clouds, and its wild beasts that roam about. And there, in a shady glen, hard by a crystal spring, the Princes of Carrión commanded that their tents be pitched, and they rested there that night with all their men, holding their wives in their arms as if with love. Ah, how ill will they requite them when the sun shines forth again!

In the morning they command that the mules be loaded with their many goods, and the tents struck where they had spent the night, and send their servants on ahead. The Princes of Carrión command that none remain behind, man or woman, save only their two wives, Doña Elvira and Doña Sol, for they think to make sport with them after their fashion.

All are now departed and the four are left alone. And now the Princes of Carrión discover their wicked plan.

"Hear us now, Doña Elvira and Doña Sol," they said. "We are going to mock you here in these wild woods and then abandon you. Never shall you see your wedding portion in the lands of Carrión! Such is the word that will come to the ears of the Cid Campeador, and thus shall we be avenged for that shame of the lion!"

They strip them then of their skins and mantles, and leave them naked save for their shifts and silken skirts. The wicked ones of Carrión now take up their spurs on their heavy thongs of leather. Their wives now see their purpose and Doña Sol pleads with them:

"In the name of God, Don Diego and Don Fernando, unsheath your swords, Colada and Tizón, so strong and sharp, and cut off our heads! Thus shall we be martyrs, and Moors and Christians will long lament your act, saying we deserved it not. Ah, do not thus cruelly misuse us! For this outrage you will be dishonored and will have to answer for it before a court of justice."

Their prayers avail them not, and the Princes of Carrión set about their work, whipping them most pitilessly with the sharp spurs and heavy thongs of leather, cutting through shifts and tender flesh, while the clean blood stains their silken skirts. Ah, what agony is theirs! And ah, if only the Cid Campeador might now appear! How wonderful that would be, God willing!

The princes whip them till they fall senseless, their garments soaked in blood. Each strives to outdo the other and they cease only when they can strike no more. Doña Elvira and Doña Sol are silent now and are left for dead there in the oaken woods of Corpes.

The princes remove their wives' mantles and

ermine skins and leave them senseless, clad only
in their shifts and silken skirts, a prey to the birds
and wild beasts of the wilderness. They leave
them there for dead, know you, and lifeless. Ah,
how wonderful it would be if the Cid Cam-
peador might now appear!

The Princes of Carrión leave them there for
dead, helpless to attend each other, and, as the
princes ride away through the forest, hear now
how they boast:

"Ha! We are now avenged for that unlucky
marriage! Not for concubines should we have
taken them, no, not even as a gift! Much too low
were they for our wedding couch! And we are
also having our revenge for that shame of the
lion!"

Thus boasted the princes, one to the other.

And now I will tell you of Félix Muñoz, that
nephew of the Cid Campeador whom the princes
had sent away, although unwillingly did he obey
them, for he felt in his heart that all was not
well with his cousins. So he withdrew from the
others and hid himself in a thicket to watch for
them, or to learn what the Princes of Carrión
had done with them. He saw the princes ap-
proaching and heard what they were saying,
although they saw him not. Had they seen him,
know you, his life had been there forfeit!

The princes spurred on and Félix Muñoz
turned back, following their tracks, and found
his cousins senseless.

"O cousins, cousins!" cried he.

He dismounted and tied his horse and spoke again:

"O my dear cousins, Doña Elvira and Doña Sol, what shameful thing is this the Princes of Carrión have done! God grant they meet their just deserts!"

He tries to awaken them, but they are in a swoon and cannot speak a word. His heart is like to break with pity and he calls to them again:

"O my cousins, Doña Elvira and Doña Sol, awake for the love of God, while it is yet day, lest in the night the wild beasts of the forest come and devour us!"

Slowly do Doña Elvira and Doña Sol return to life. They open their eyes and see Félix Muñoz.

"Courage, my cousins!" he cried. "For the love of God! When the Princes of Carrión discover my absence they will return hither in all haste to seek me, and then, unless God help us, here shall we die!"

Then up spoke Doña Sol, and painfully spoke she:

"May the Campeador reward you as you deserve! Give us water for the love of God!"

In his hat, clean and new, which he had brought from Valencia, Félix Muñoz fetches water from the spring. Badly are they wounded and he lets them drink their fill.

They rise at last as he has urged. He comforts them and gives them courage, and they take heart. Then he puts them upon his horse and covers them with his mantle, and leading his horse he hastens thence. All that day he follows the paths through the oaken woods of Corpes, and the three emerge at nightfall upon the banks of the Duero. And there, in the Castle of Doña Urraca, Félix Muñoz leaves them and rides away to San Esteban, where Diego Téllez is, a vassal of Alvar Fáñez.

Diego Téllez heard his tale and bitterly did he grieve. With horses and noble garments he rode forth at once to seek Doña Elvira and Doña Sol, whom he brought in all honor back to San Esteban. Those of San Esteban, good people all, were much afflicted and offered the daughters of the Cid the fruits of their tribute, and there did the Cid's daughters tarry until they had recovered.

The Princes of Carrión went their way boasting one to the other, but in all the land their deed was soon known, and good King Alfonso was grieved in his heart. Word of it reached Valencia the great, and when My Cid heard it he stood a long hour in thought, and then he grasped his beard and swore:

"All praise to Jesus Christ Our Lord! The Princes of Carrión have done this shameful thing to me, but by this beard which none has ever touched, they shall not dishonor me! I shall yet marry my daughters well!"

My Cid was grieved, and all his court was also, and Alvar Fáñez was stricken to the heart. Minaya then mounted, with him Pedro Bermúdez and Martín Antolínez, that noble son of Burgos, and two hundred of My Cid's company, and all were commanded by My Cid to ride night and day and bring his daughters back to great Valencia.

They tarried not, but obeyed their lord's command and galloped forth and rode day and night to Gormaz, that strong castle, where they rested a single night.

Word reached San Esteban that Minaya was coming to fetch his two cousins, and the knights of San Esteban, like the noblemen they were, received Minaya and his men. They offered Minaya the fruits of their tribute, but he took them not, although he thanked them, saying:

"I am obliged to you, O knights of San Esteban, prudent men that you are, for this honor that you do us, and My Cid the Campeador, there in Valencia, will thank you likewise, as I do in his name. God in His heaven grant that you have your reward!"

All, well pleased, thanked him for his words and retired to rest.

Minaya then went to seek his cousins, Doña Elvira and Doña Sol, who saw him and cried:

"Ah, we are as happy to see you as if you were God himself! And you may thank Him that you find us alive! Some idle day in great Valencia we will tell you the tale of our misfortunes."

They and Alvar Fáñez wept, and Pedro Bermúdez wept also and said:

"Doña Elvira and Doña Sol, be of good cheer, for you are safe and well and no harm can come to you. You have lost a good marriage, but you shall have a better! And may we soon see the day when we can avenge you!"

They rest there very joyfully that night and the next day in the morning they mount. Those of San Esteban escort them to the River Amor, comforting them. There they take their leave and turn back, and Minaya rides on with the ladies.

They cross the Alcoceba by the ford of Vadorrey, leaving the castle of Gormaz to their right, and rest at the town of Berlanga. In the morning they ride again and stop that night at Medina, and another day finds them at Molina.

The Moor Abengalbón, well pleased, rode gladly forth to welcome them, and for the love he bore My Cid he offered them a rich supper. Thence they straightway set out for Valencia.

He who in a happy hour was born heard that they were coming and swiftly spurred to meet them, doing mock battle the while because of his great joy. My Cid embraced his daughters and kissed them both, and smiled again, saying:

"And have you returned, my daughters? May God keep you from harm! I it was who accepted your marriage, for I dared not do otherwise. But now, please God, I shall see you better wed! And God grant me vengeance upon my sons-in-law, the Princes of Carrión!"

The daughters kissed their father's hands, and all joyfully entered the city, where Doña Ximena rejoiced with them.

He who in a happy hour was born tarried not, but called his men to council, thinking to send a message to King Alfonso.

"Where are you, Muño Gustioz, my noble vassal?" he cried. "It was a lucky day for me when I brought you to my court! Take you now this message to King Alfonso in Castile and kiss his hands for me most lovingly, for I am his vassal, as he is my lord. Tell the good King to weigh in his heart this wrong which the Princes of Carrión have done to us, for he it was who gave my daughters in marriage, not I, and they have been basely abandoned. Some dishonor falls to us therefrom, but, great or small, it is all dishonor for the King. The Princes of Carrión have also taken of me vast riches, which I resent, along with the shameful thing they did. Let the King be their judge and summon them to trial before their peers, or before his court of justice, that the Princes of Carrión may right the wrong they have done me, for great is the anger I bear them in my heart."

Muño Gustioz mounted forthwith, in his company two knights who gladly served him, and certain squires of My Cid's household. They rode forth from Valencia, resting not, day or night. They found the King at Sahagún.

King of Castile is he, and of León, and Asturias and Oviedo! Lord is he likewise of Santiago de Compostela, and the Counts of Galicia do him homage!

Muño Gustioz dismounted and did reverence to the saints of heaven and said a prayer to God. Which done, with the two knights of his escort he went to the palace, where the King was hold-

ing his court. They entered, and the King knew
Muño Gustioz at once, and even rose to his feet,
so happy was he to receive him. Then did Muño
Gustioz kneel before the King and kiss his feet.

"A boon, O King, lord of these wide domains!"
he cried. "The Campeador kisses your feet and
hands, for he is your vassal, as you are his lord.
You it was who gave the hands of his daughters
to the Princes of Carrión, for you desired a high
marriage for them. Now you know how great is
the honor which the Princes have brought us!
How they have besmirched us! How they have
outraged the daughters of the Cid Campeador!
For they abandoned them, beaten and naked
and shamed, in the oaken woods of Corpes,
exposed to the wild beasts and birds of the wil-
derness! His daughters are now with him in
Valencia. Therefore, O King, he kisses your hands
and begs you to bring the Princes of Carrión
before their peers, or before your court of jus-
tice. He holds himself dishonored, but your dis-
honor, O King, is far greater than his! My Cid
begs that you, who know all this, join him in his
suit and give him justice of the Princes of Car-
rión."

For a long hour the King was silent, and then
he said:

"I tell you truly that I am grieved in my heart
and that what you say, Muño Gustioz, is fact,
for I it was who gave My Cid's daughters to the
Princes of Carrión. I meant it well, for their
honor. Would that that union had never been! I

share the grief of My Cid and I shall give him justice, with the help of God! Little did I reck what I was doing! I shall send my heralds forth to all parts of my kingdom to announce that my court of justice will be held in Toledo, and let all my counts and knights attend it. And I shall command that the Princes of Carrión appear there also, to answer the charges of My Cid the Campeador. He shall suffer no wrong if it is in my power to prevent it! And tell the Cid Campeador, he who in a happy hour was born, to come with his vassals to Toledo within seven weeks. This is the term I set. I shall hold this court for the love I bear My Cid. Salute him and his for me and let them be comforted, for they shall yet gain honor from their misfortunes."

Muño Gustioz then took his leave of the King and returned to My Cid.

As Alfonso the Castilian has said, so does he do, for he takes the Cid's suit as his own, sending his edict to León and Santiago de Compostela, to the nobles of Portugal and Galicia, and to those of Carrión and Castile, announcing that the honest King will hold his court of justice in Toledo, and bidding them foregather there within seven weeks. Furthermore, he warns that all who fail to attend will no longer be his vassals. Throughout all the kingdom his mandate is obeyed.

The Princes of Carrión were troubled by this court that the King had called in Toledo, for they feared that My Cid the Campeador would be there. So with the counsel of their kinsmen they begged the King to excuse them from attending, but the King made answer, saying:

"God save us! That I will not do! My Cid the Campeador will be there, and you shall answer the charges that he makes against you. He who refuses to attend my court, let him leave my kingdom, for I shall love him not!"

Now do the Princes of Carrión know they cannot escape, and they again take counsel with their kinsmen. Count García, that enemy of My Cid who has always sought to do him hurt, here intervenes and lends his counsel to the Princes of Carrión.

The term draws to its close and all come to the court, among the first the good King Alfonso, and Count Enrique, and Count Ramón, father of the good emperor, and Count Fruela and Count Birbón. And many other learned men from all the kingdom do gather there, the best of Castile. Count García also comes, he who is called El Crespo de Grañón, and Alvar Díaz, he who commanded at Oca, and Asur González, and Gonzalo Ansúrez, and Pedro Ansúrez. Diego and Fernando fail not, but bring with them a great company to the court, thinking perhaps they may harm the Cid Campeador.

Now they are gathered from all parts, but My Cid does not arrive, displeasing the King thereby. Upon the fifth day My Cid the Campeador appears, having sent before him Alvar Fáñez to kiss the hands of the King his lord and to announce that he will arrive that night.

The King heard and rejoiced, and set out with many of his men to receive him who in a happy hour was born.

The Cid and his great company, fitting for such a lord, arrive in splendid array. When they come into the presence of the good King Alfonso My Cid alights and prostrates himself in honor of his lord. But the King at once protests, saying:

"By St. Isidore, this I will not permit! Mount again, O Cid, or I shall be displeased. Let us kiss each other from our hearts, for your grievance is also mine. God grant that my court honor itself this day by doing you justice!"

My Cid the good Campeador kissed the King's hands and then his mouth.

"Amen!" he said. "God be thanked that I see you again, my lord! I salute you and Count Ramón, and Count Enrique, and all those here present. God be with our friends, and with you most of all, my lord! My noble wife Doña Ximena sends her greetings, as do my two daughters, and begs that you share their grief, my lord."

"That I shall, with the help of God!" replied the King.

The King turned back to Toledo, but My Cid wished not to cross the Tagus that night.

"A boon, O King, and God save you!" he said. "Do you, my lord, enter into the city, while I

rest at San Servando with my men, for my com-
panies will arrive this night and I wish to keep
vigil in this holy place. Tomorrow I will enter
the city and come to your court before I break
my fast."

"Be it so," said the King.

King Alfonso then entered Toledo and My Cid
Ruy Díaz rested at San Servando, where he com-
manded that lamps be lighted and set upon the
altar, for he wished to keep vigil in that holy
place and pray to God in secret.

Minaya and his good men were ready when
morning came. Matins and early Mass were said
before the sun shone forth, and a noble offering
was made.

"Minaya Alvar Fáñez, my right arm," said
My Cid, "do you come with me and bring Bishop
Jerome and Pedro Bermúdez, and Muño Gustioz,
and Martín Antolínez, that noble son of Burgos,
and Alvar Alvarez, and Alvar Salvadórez, and
Martín Muñoz, born under a lucky star, and
my nephew Félix Muñoz. And I will bring with
me the wise Mal Anda, and Galindo García, the
good Aragonese, and as many more of our men
as will make a company of a hundred. Let them
don their quilted tunics, lest their armor chafe
them, and over their tunics their coats of mail,
shining like the sun. Above their armor they
will wear their ermines and other skins, the
latches well fastened. And under their mantles
let them gird on their sweet-cutting swords. In
such wise shall we arrive at the court to demand
justice and plead our cause. Then, if those of

Carrión seek trouble, well, with a hundred knights like these I shall fear them not!"

"We are with you, my lord!" replied his men.

As the Cid has commanded, so do they attire themselves.

He tarries not, but dons his good cloth hose, his shoes embroidered with golden threads, and his linen shirt, white as the sun, its fastenings all of gold and silver, its cuffs likewise embroidered, over it a tunic worked with glistening gold, and then the vermilion skin with the golden fringe which My Cid wears always. A linen cap shot with gold covers the head of My Cid the Campeador, lest a single hair be touched. He fails not to bind his great beard also with a cord, for thus he guards his person against mischance. Finally, he casts about his shoulders a mantle of such great price that all who behold it are astonished.

Thus with his hundred, all attired as he has commanded, My Cid rides swiftly from San Servando to the court. He alights at the outer gate and enters with all his men, he in their midst, the hundred surrounding him.

King Alfonso sees him enter and stands, and Count Enrique and Count Ramón, and, know you, all the others of the court stand also. With such honor do they receive him who in a happy hour was born! But El Crespo de Grañón rises not, nor do those of the party of the Princes of Carrión. The King then grasps the hand of My Cid and says:

"O Campeador, sit you here with me upon this

bench which you gave me. Some of those pres-
ent will like it not, but I say you are a better man
than we!"

He who won Valencia thanked the King and
said:

"No, my lord. That is your place as our King
and lord. I will sit here with my men."

The King was pleased with the words of My
Cid, who sat upon his carved bench in the midst
of those who guarded him.

All the court gazed upon My Cid, upon his
great beard bound with its cord, and he seemed
to them a perfect knight in very truth. But the
Princes of Carrión, for shame, would not look
upon him.

Then good King Alfonso rose to his feet and
said:

"Hear me now, my companions, and God save
you! Since I was made King but two courts of
justice have I held, the one at Burgos, the other
at Carrión. This third court at Toledo I have
called today for love of My Cid, he who in a
happy hour was born, that he receive justice of
the Princes of Carrión, for they have wronged
him grievously, as all the world knows. As judges
of this court I hereby name Count Enrique and
Count Ramón, and all these other counts who
are not of the party of Carrión. Think upon this
case which is known to you and decide where
justice lies, for injustice I will not tolerate. And
let both parties keep the peace this day, for I
swear by St. Isidore that he who disturbs my
court shall be banished from my kingdom and

my love! I shall be with him whose cause is just. And now let My Cid the Campeador prefer his charges and we shall see what reply the Princes of Carrión will make."

My Cid kissed the King's hands and rose to his feet.

"Much do I thank you, my King and lord," he said, "for this court which you have called on my behalf. These are the charges I make against the Princes of Carrión. It was not I who was dishonored by their abandonment of my daughters, but you, O King, who gave their hands in marriage, and you will know what you must do this day. When my sons-in-law brought my daughters from great Valencia I did truly love them and gave them my swords Colada and Tizón, which I had won in equal battle, that they might gain honor with them and serve you, O King. But they abandoned my daughters in the oaken woods of Corpes and clearly showed they wanted naught of mine, and thus they lost my love. Therefore let them give me back my swords, for they are my sons-in-law no longer."

"This is right," said the judges.

Then said Count García to the Princes of Carrión:

"Let us answer him."

Those of Carrión then withdrew with the kinsmen and their party quickly formed their argument, thus:

"The Cid Campeador shows us favor by not charging us with the dishonor of his daughters. With the King's permission, then, let us offer him an arrangement, returning the swords he claims as his. And then let him depart hence, for the Cid Campeador will no longer have a case against us."

The Princes of Carrión then returned and said:

"A boon, King Alfonso, our lord! We do not deny that he gave us his swords, and, since he now claims them, we hereby yield them to him in your presence."

Whereupon they gave Colada and Tizón into the hands of the King their lord, who then unsheathed them, dazzling all the court, for the hilts and guards were of purest gold. The King gave the swords to My Cid, who received them and kissed the King's hands and returned to the bench whence he had arisen.

My Cid took the swords in his hands and closely did he scan them. He saw they were the same, for well did he know them, and he rejoiced in his whole body and smiled happily. Then he raised his hand to his beard and swore:

"By this beard which none has ever touched, Doña Elvira and Doña Sol shall be avenged!"

Then he called his nephew Pedro Bermúdez to him and put Tizón into his hands, saying:

"Take it, my nephew, for now it will have a better master!"

To Martín Antolínez, that noble son of Burgos, he gave his sword Colada and said:

"Martín Antolínez, my excellent vassal, do you take Colada, which I won from its good master, Ramón Berenguer of great Barcelona. It is now yours. Guard it well, for I know that when need arises you will win with it great fame and honor."

Martín Antolínez took the sword and kissed the hands of My Cid the Campeador, who then arose and said:

"I thank God and you, my King and lord! My swords Colada and Tizón have been restored, but I have yet another charge to make against the Princes of Carrión. When they brought my daughters from Valencia I made them a present of three thousand marks, and for this act of mine they repaid me as you know. Let them return my money, because they are my sons-in-law no longer."

Ah, you should have heard the outcry of the Princes of Carrión. Count Ramón reproved them, saying:

"Make your answer yes or no!"

Then replied the Princes of Carrión:

"We yielded up his swords to the Cid Campeador to the end that he demand no more of us."

Then said Count Ramón:

"If it please the King, our judgment is that you, O King, decide the matter."

Said the good King:

"I find in favor of My Cid."

Then uprose the Cid Campeador and said to the Princes of Carrión:

"This money that I gave you, let me have it now, or do you make an accounting of it."

The Princes of Carrión again withdrew for counsel, but found no answer, for great was the sum and they had spent it all. So they returned and said:

"He who won Valencia presses us sorely, so greedy he for our wealth, but we will pay him from our estate in the lands of Carrión."

Thus they acknowledged their debt, and the judges said:

"If the Cid will accept this arrangement we will not forbid it, but our judgment is, and we so command, that the money be delivered to him in the presence of this court."

Then said King Alfonso:

"We recognize the demand of the Cid Campeador as right and lawful. Of his three thousand marks I have two hundred which the Princes of Carrión gave me for a present. I hereby return them to the princes, for they are now ruined men, and let them give the money to My Cid, he who in a happy hour was born, for I want it not."

Then up spoke Fernando González. Hear now what he said:

"Coined money have we none."

And Count Ramón replied:

"Since you have spent the gold and silver, our judgment, which we pronounce in the presence of the King, is that you pay in kind, and let the Campeador be satisfied with this."

Now the Princes of Carrión do plainly see they have no choice but to obey. Ah, you should have seen them bringing all those swift war horses, all those sleek mules, all those noble palfreys, all those richly wrought swords! And as the court sums up their worth, My Cid receives it all. The Princes of Carrión thus pay their debt, giving over the two hundred marks of King Alfonso and borrowing what they have not of their own. In this judgment, know you, they come off very badly.

My Cid accepts the payment and his men hold and guard it. Which done, My Cid makes yet another charge, saying:

"A boon, O King and lord, for love and charity! I cannot omit my most grievous wrong. Hear me, all the court, and share my wrath! Because of it I hereby challenge to single combat the Princes of Carrión who thus dishonored me! Tell me now, O Princes of Carrión, what have I ever done to you that you should treat me thus? Here in the presence of the King I demand justice of you. Why did you rend the very stuff of my heart? I yielded you my daughters when you left Valencia and did you great honor and gave you great gifts. If you loved them not, treacherous curs that you are, why did you bring them and their goods from Valencia? Why did you whip them with spurs? And why did you abandon them in the oaken woods of Corpes, abandon them to the wild beasts and birds of the wilderness? Thus did you bring infamy upon yourselves! Let the court say whether you owe me satisfaction."

Then uprose Count García and said:

"A boon, O best of kings! How well prepared has My Cid come to this court, he with his great beard! Some have fear of him, others he frightens with it. But I say that the Princes of Carrión are of such lofty estate that they should not have taken his daughters even for concubines, much less as wives and equals! What nonsense is this! They did well to abandon them, I say! We care not a fig for his charges!"

Then did the Campeador grasp his beard and say:

"Now God be praised who rules heaven and earth! My beard is long because it was grown with love. Count, what have you to cast in this beard of mine which I have nourished with such delight since first it sprouted? Never did man born of woman, Moor or Christian, pluck it as I did yours, O count, at the castle of Cabra! When I took Cabra and plucked your beard, there was no youth but took his share of it! And what I plucked has not grown back again, for here I have it in my wallet!"

At this Fernando González sprang to his feet, shouting. Hear now what he said:

"Forbear, O Cid! You have been paid. Let there be no further quarrel between us, for we are by birth the Princes of Carrión, a fitting match for the daughters of kings or emperors, not those of mere knights! When we abandoned your daughters we did only what was our right, and did ourselves no dishonor thereby, but honor!"

Then glanced My Cid at Pedro Bermúdez and said:

"Speak now, Mute Pedro, O silent one! My daughters are your blood cousins. I am the one addressed, but you it is whose ears are pulled! If I reply you may not challenge them."

Pedro Bermúdez attempts to speak, but his tongue is tied and no words come; but, know you, when he does begin he cannot stop.

"You have strange ways with me, O Cid!" he said. "Always in your court do you call me Mute Pedro, and well you know I cannot suffer it! But what I must do, that shall I do!

"You lie, Fernando! In every word you lie! What you are you owe the Campeador. And now let me speak a little of your fine deeds. Do you not remember that day we fought the Moors near great Valencia? That day you begged of the loyal Campeador the honor of striking the first blow? That day you saw a Moor and set upon him, but turned tail and fled before you touched him? Had I not been there the Moor had served you well! I rode between you and felled him with one blow, and gave you his horse and kept your secret. Not until this day have I revealed it. And you, what did you then? Why, you boasted to My Cid and all the world how you had slain the Moor in that great battle! And they believed you, but they knew not the truth. A comely youth you are, but a craven! Tongue without hands! How dare you speak?

"Tell me now, Fernando, do you not remember also that matter of the lion there in Valencia, when My Cid was sleeping and the lion escaped? And you, Fernando, what did you in your great fear? Why, you hid beneath the bench of My Cid the Campeador! You hid, Fernando, and brought dishonor upon yourself! We surrounded the bench to protect our lord. Then My Cid awoke, he who won Valencia, and arose and approached the lion. And the lion lowered his head and let My Cid take him by the mane and lead him back to his cage. My Cid then turned to his vassals who were standing roundabout and inquired for his sons-in-law, but neither could be found. Therefore do I challenge you for a treacherous villain, and in the name of the Cid's daughters I shall fight you in the presence of King Alfonso. You abandoned them, like the faithless villains that you are! They are but women, but in every respect your betters, and when I meet you, God willing, you shall confess yourself a scoundrel! And what I say here I shall defend!"

Then up spoke Diego González. Hear now what he said:

"By birth we are the Princes of Carrión. Would to God this marriage had never been! Thus we had not been kinsmen of My Cid Don Rodrigo! We repent not of having abandoned his daughters, let them sigh as they will so long as they shall live! The insult that we offered them will be cast in their faces, for we did ourselves honor by abandoning them, and this I shall defend in mortal combat!"

Behold now Martín Antolínez who stood and shouted:

"Hold your lying tongue, shameless one! When will you forget that affair of the lion? Why, you ran out into the stable yard and hid yourself be-

hind the wine press! That silken tunic of yours
will never be worn again! And this I shall defend
in combat: that the daughters of the Cid whom
you abandoned are in every way your betters!
And when we meet you shall confess by your
own mouth that you are a perfidious dog and
utter naught but lies!"

At this point in the dispute, Asur González,
his long ermine robe trailing behind him, entered
the court. His face was crimson, for he had just
dined, and what he said was folly.

"O my lords, when was such nonsense ever
heard! How could My Cid, he of Bivar, bring
honor to us? Let him go back to his mills on the
Ubierna and dress his millstones and grind his
grist, as he used! Who could have put it into his
head that he might marry into the family of
Carrión!"

Then arose Muño Gustioz and said:

"Have done, O man of little shame! Faithless
villain that you are! You who dine before your
prayers and with your stinking breath turn the
stomachs of those you kiss! You who lie to
friend and lord! False to everyone and most of
all to God! I want no part of your friendship
and I shall make you confess that you are every-
thing I say!"

Then up spoke King Alfonso and said:

"Enough of this! Those who have thus defied
each other shall fight, so help me God!"

The arguments are ended, and now behold two
knights who enter the court, the one named

Ojarra, the other Iñigo Ximénez; the first the ambassador of the Prince of Navarre, the second, that of the Prince of Aragón. They kiss the hands of King Alfonso and beg of the Cid that he give, with his blessing, the hands of his daughters in marriage, to be queens of Navarre and Aragón. Now indeed did silence fall upon the court, and My Cid the Campeador rose to his feet and said:

"A boon, King Alfonso my lord! I thank God that my daughters are sought in marriage in Aragón and Navarre! You it was who wed them once, not I, and now I give them once again into your hands, for without your consent I shall do nothing."

The King arose and commanded silence in the court.

"I pray you, noble Cid, O illustrious Campeador," he said, "to accept this offer. You have my consent. And let the marriage be authorized by this very court, for thus shall we gain in lands and honor."

The Cid stood and kissed the King's hands.

"If such be your desire, my lord," he said, "I also give my consent."

Then said the King:

"May God reward you! Ojarra and Iñigo Ximénez, I hereby consent to the lawful marriage of the daughters of My Cid, Doña Elvira and Doña Sol, to the princes of Navarre and Aragón, and they have my blessing."

Ojarra and Iñigo Ximénez arose and kissed the hands of King Alfonso and My Cid the Campeador. Word was given and oath taken that what was there agreed would be fulfilled and even surpassed, which pleased many at the court, although it pleased not the Princes of Carrión.

Alvar Fáñez then arose and said:

"I beg a boon of you, my King and lord, and let it not displease the Cid Campeador. I have listened to the arguments of the others before this court and would now say something of my own."

"Speak," said the King. "Say what you will, Minaya."

"I beg the court to hear me," said Minaya, "for I have a bitter charge to make against the Princes of Carrión. Acting for my King Alfonso, I it was who gave my cousins to wed, and the princes took them to be their lawful wives. Vast was the dowry that My Cid the Campeador gave them, and the princes abandoned them, to our great sorrow. Therefore do I challenge them to single combat for the faithless rascals that they are! You, O princes, are of the blood of the Beni-Gómez, which has given us counts of honor and courage, but well we know how it has fallen! I thank God that the princes of Navarre and Aragón seek the hands of my cousins, Doña Elvira and Doña Sol! Once you held them in your arms as equals; now you will kiss their hands and call them 'highness'! And you will serve them, whether you like it or not! I thank God, I say, and my lord King Alfonso, for thus will the honor of My Cid the Campeador be increased! I have told you what you are, O princes, and if any would gainsay me, here stands Alvar Fáñez, as good as the best!"

At this Gómez Peláez arose and said:

"What mean those vain words, Minaya? In this court are many who are your match, let him deny it who dares! And if it please God that we should win this suit, then you shall see whether or not I speak the truth!"

"No more of this!" said the King. "Not another word! Tomorrow at sunrise these six shall fight, three to three, as they have defied each other in this court."

Then up spoke the Princes of Carrión and said:

"Give us more time, O King, for we cannot fight tomorrow. We have yielded up our horses and our arms to the Campeador and will have to seek others in the lands of Carrión."

Said the King to the Campeador:

"Let the combat be where you wish."

"My lord," replied the Cid, "I would not fight in the lands of Carrión, but would return to Valencia."

"Be it as you wish, Campeador," said the King. "Give me your knights, then, all armed, and let them go with me, and I shall protect them. This I undertake, as a lord for his vassals, lest they suffer violence at the hands of count or knight. And now, here in this court, I set the time and place of combat at three weeks hence in the fields of Carrión, and let the combat be in my presence. He who fails to appear shall lose his cause and be judged vanquished and faithless."

The Princes of Carrión accepted the King's mandate.

My Cid then kissed the hands of the King and said:

"These three knights of mine I give into your power. I commend them to you as my King and lord. They will do their duty. And do you send them back to me, with honor, to Valencia, for the love of God!"

"God grant it!" replied the King.

The Cid Campeador then doffed his helmet and his linen cap, white and shining as the sun, and loosed the cord which bound his beard, while all the court gazed in wonder. He embraced Count Enrique and Count Ramón and begged them to take of his goods what they would. He did the same with all those of his party, and some did take and others not. He also forgave the King his two hundred marks and of the rest took only what he needed. And then he said:

"A boon, O King, for the love of God! Now that our suit is settled, I kiss your hands, my lord, and beg your leave to depart for Valencia, which I won at such great cost."

[Then My Cid commanded that the ambassadors of the princes of Navarre and Aragón be given horses and whatever they might need, and bade them farewell.

King Alfonso mounted with all the nobles of his court and escorted the Cid beyond the city. My Cid was riding Babieca his horse when they came to Zocodover, and the King said to him:

"Don Rodrigo, by the obedience you owe me, will you not run that horse of yours of which I have heard such marvelous things?"

The Cid smiled and said:

"My lord, here in your court are many famous men, well mounted. Do you command them to ride for you."

"O Cid," replied the King, "what you say is true, but still, if you love me, let your horse run for me."

The Cid then put spurs to Babieca and so swiftly did he ride that all were astonished.]

Whereupon the King raised his right hand and crossed himself, saying:

"I swear by St. Isidore of León, there is not another such knight in all our lands!"

My Cid then rode up to his lord King Alfonso and kissed his hands.

"You commanded me, O King," he said, "to display what Babieca the swift can do. There is not his equal among Moors or Christians! He is yours, my lord! Pray accept him."

"That I will not!" replied the King. "If I should take him the horse would not have such a good master. For a horse like Babieca a rider like you, to drive the Moors from the battlefield and pursue them! May God withhold His love from him who would take Babieca from you, for you and he have brought us much honor!"

At this they took their leave of one another and the court departed. The Campeador then instructed the three who were to fight for him, saying:

"Now, Martín Antolínez and you, Pedro Bermúdez, and you, Muño Gustioz, my noble vassal, stand you firm on the field like the good knights that you are, and let me hear pleasant things of you there in Valencia."

"Why say you this, my lord?" replied Martín Antolínez. "We have taken up your debt and we shall pay it. You may hear, indeed, that we are dead, but vanquished, never!"

Joyfully heard he these words, he who in a happy hour was born, and bade farewell to his friends.

The Cid departed then for Valencia, the King for Carrión.

The three weeks of the term have now expired, and behold now the Cid's men who go to meet their obligation, as their lord has commanded, under the protection of Alfonso, he of León. Two days do they await the Princes of Carrión, who come well mounted and well armed. The princes and their kinsmen think to lure the Cid's men away and slay them if they can, to dishonor My Cid their lord. This is a wicked thing, but they dare not do it, so great their fear of Alfonso, he of León.

That night My Cid's men keep vigil over their arms and pray. The night passes and dawn shines forth. Many are the good nobles who come joyfully to the combat, and the greatest of them, King Alfonso, is also there to see that all is lawfully done, without fraud or treachery.

Now those of My Cid don their armor, all

three as one, in defense of their lord. In another spot the Princes of Carrión also arm themselves, but Count García counsels them to protest to King Alfonso and beg him to forbid those of the Campeador to bring Colada and Tizón into the combat, for bitterly do the princes regret having had to yield them up. Thus do they petition the King, but he will not consent and says:

"When we held our court you made no such exception. If your swords are good they will serve you well. Those of the Campeador's men will do likewise. So get you to the field, O Princes of Carrión, and fight like men, for those of the Campeador will not fail you. If you win this day, great will be your honor; but if you lose, blame me not, for well you know this quarrel was of your seeking."

Now indeed do the Princes of Carrión repent what they have done and would give all their lands of Carrión could they undo it.

Those of the Campeador, all three, are now in armor, and King Alfonso inspects them as they thus address him:

"We kiss your hands, O King and lord, and beg that you be judge this day between us and them. Let your law prevail and permit no injustice, for the Princes of Carrión have brought their men with them and we know not what they have in mind to do. Our lord the Cid entrusted us to you, O King, and your law is our protection."

"That it shall be!" replied the King.

Their horses are now led forth, so good and

swift, and they make the sign of the Cross upon their saddles and quickly mount, their shields with the golden bosses hanging from their necks, in their hands their sharp lances, each with its pennant, and many good knights go with them. Now they ride into the field where the lists are, and all vow, these men of the Campeador, that each will strike his man.

On the other side behold the Princes of Carrión, surrounded by their many kinsmen. The King names umpires to tell them what is lawful and what is not, and forbids them to dispute the decisions. Then they ride forth upon the field and King Alfonso says to them:

"Hear me now, O Princes of Carrión. This combat was to have been in Toledo, but you wished it not, so I have brought these three knights of My Cid the Campeador under my protection to the lands of Carrión. See that you obey the law and do them no hurt, for he who harms them will no longer be welcome in my kingdom."

How regretful now are the Princes of Carrión!

The King and his umpires place the lists and leave the field, and warn that those who leave the lists will be judged vanquished. All the people are removed three lance lengths away.

Now the field is divided so that none will face the sun. The umpires withdraw and the combatants are face to face. Those of My Cid ride against the Princes of Carrión, and these against the men of the Campeador, each watching his adversary. All hold their shields before their breasts, lower their lances, pennants flying, lean forward in their saddles, and spur their horses. Ah, how the earth trembles at their charge! Each keeps his eyes upon his man, and all, three against three, collide, and those who watch them think that none can escape alive.

Pedro Bermúdez, the first of the challengers, rides against Fernando González, and they strike each other's shields most fearlessly. The lance of Fernando pierces Pedro's shield, but touches not his flesh, and breaks. Firm stands Pedro Bermúdez and yields not, but gives as good as he takes, striking through the boss of the other's shield, which now protects him not. He strikes him in the breast, near the heart, piercing two of the three coats of mail that Fernando wears. Two does he pierce, but the third one holds, although it is forced a handbreadth into the flesh, together with the quilted tunic and rings of mail. Blood pours from Fernando's mouth. His cinches give and he falls over his horse's crupper to the ground. All think he is surely wounded unto death. Then does Pedro Bermúdez drop his lance and grasp his sword. Fernando knows Tizón and waits not for the blow to fall, but cries:

"I yield, I yield!"

The umpires so certify and Pedro Bermúdez rides from the lists.

Then do Don Martín and Diego González have at each other, dealing blows that shiver their lances. Martín Antolínez then draws Colada, so shining bright that it lights up all the field, and strikes. He cuts the straps of Don Diego's helmet and knocks it to the ground, where all the pieces roll about. Colada cuts through the cap, shears the hair, and touches the flesh. With this one blow struck by Colada the precious, Diego González sees that he cannot escape with his life and turns his horse's head. His sword is in his hand, but he dares not use it. And now Martín Antolínez attacks and strikes, not with the edge of his blade, but with its flat. Hear now how the prince cries out:

"Help me, O glorious God! Save me from his sword, O Lord!"

He turns his horse to avoid the blade and flies the lists, leaving the field to Don Martín. Then said the King:

"Come to my side, Don Martín, for you have won the combat."

The umpires judge that the King has spoken truly.

These two have won their victories, and now I will tell you of Muño Gustioz, how he fought with Asur González. Heavy are the blows they take upon their shields. Asur González is a valorous man and strong, and he strikes Muño Gustioz upon the shield and pierces it and the mail beneath, but wounds him not. Then in turn does Muño Gustioz strike the boss of the other's shield. Asur cannot parry the thrust and it pierces mail and flesh, but touches not his heart. Lance and pennant pierce the flesh and protrude a fathom's length beyond. Muño then twists his lance and knocks Asur from his saddle to the ground. Red are shaft and lance and pennant, and all believe him slain. Muño then retrieves his lance and stands above his enemy, but Gonzalo Ansúrez shouts:

"Strike him not, for the love of God! You have won the field! Let this be the end!"

The umpires so certify.

Then does good King Alfonso command that the field be cleared and takes the arms that there remain. The men of the good Campeador depart full of honor, for they have won the day, God be thanked! But great is the grief in the lands of Carrión!

Happy is My Cid the Campeador! Shamed are the Princes of Carrión! He who abuses a good wife and then abandons her, let such always be his fate, or worse!

Let us now leave the Princes of Carrión, who are bitter at their punishment, and speak of him who in a happy hour was born. Great is the rejoicing in noble Valencia at the honor won by those of the Campeador. Ruy Díaz, their lord, grasps his beard and thus addresses them:

"I thank God, King of heaven, that my daughters are now avenged. Now they are quit of the lands of Carrión and I can give their hands in marriage, without shame, in spite of all the world!"

Those of Navarre and Aragón make their petition to Alfonso, he of León, and Doña Elvira

and Doña Sol are wed again. Great was their
first marriage feast, but this is greater far, and
brings more honor to their household. See how
his honor increases, he who in a happy hour was
born, for the Kings of Spain are now among his
kinsmen!

My Cid, lord of Valencia, passed from this life
on the Day of Pentecost. May Our Lord Jesus
have mercy on his soul! And may His mercy be
with all of us, the righteous and the sinners
equally!

Such were the deeds of My Cid the Campeador,
and this is the end of my song.